The Big Vocabulary Play Book

for
Gifted & Talented
Children

Ages 9 and up

Liz Judge

Copyright © 2020 Liz Judge
All rights reserved.

This book may be photocopied, to use in schools or the home with the student(s) for which it was purchased, but may not be reproduced in any other form without the prior permission in writing from the publishers.

contact: liz.judge55@gmail.com

INTRODUCTION

The young gifted child has a plethora of opportunities to stimulate their natural curiosity toward new words. Many amaze and amuse us as young fluent readers, as they enjoy and discover language. One of the challenges in their insatiable thirst for knowledge, however, is developing an advanced vocabulary, so that they are able to read and comprehend higher level texts.

This book has been created for parents or teachers to work with their children to expand their knowledge of higher level vocabulary. The exercises and games have been designed to be more fun and entertaining than word lists, or standard flash cards by themselves. Although some of the activities can be done on their own, the main emphasis is to have a varied set of exercises that are engaging and memorable.

Whether learning new words for general knowledge, or studying for advanced placement tests, we hope that *The Big Vocabulary Play Book* will be a valued resource in your child's educational journey.

Liz Judge
April 2020

HOW TO USE THIS BOOK

ALL YOU NEED:

Pencils, scissors, dice, and occasionally, a little glue (or tape, if you will)

This book is about learning and effectively memorizing, it is not about testing what is not yet learnt. That being the case, there is no cheating; the glossary and answer key are intended to help, and looking up words is encouraged.

The book provides 52 different activities so that you will have not only variety, but also exercises that are of different lengths and levels of ability (Beginner, Advanced, and Expert). They may be used in any order, and the opportunity to photocopy allows the child to revisit vocabulary through games and puzzles as often as they wish.

Using this book, your child can expect to learn twenty or more new words each week without it becoming a chore. As they learn, they will "magically" come across words in their reading and everyday life that before they had not noticed, skipped over through lack of understanding, or simply misinterpreted. Now is the time to advise your child to use this vocabulary as often as possible.

You will notice that some vocabulary is repeated and some activities have more words than others. This is to refresh and provide thematic links that will support learning. Encourage your child to use the pages at the back of the book to practice new words. There is no need to be boring – maybe they like to use bubble writing, create a border of synonyms, make up funny sentences or draw pictures of words. These are all effective ways of learning.

Contents

1.	Missing Link	Beginner	Pg. 8
2.	Analogies	Advanced	Pg. 9
3.	You're Breaking Up	Beginner	Pg. 10
4.	Fake News	Advanced	Pg. 12
5.	Word Search I - Synonyms	Advanced	Pg. 14
6.	Snakes 'N Ladders	Advanced	Pg. 16
7.	Shop 'Til You Drop	Advanced	Pg. 22
8.	Synonyms In The Wild	Expert	Pg. 24
9.	Where Am I?	Beginner	Pg. 26
10.	Funny Faces	Advanced	Pg. 30
11.	Fill In The Blank	Expert	Pg. 35
12.	Word Ladders	Beginner	Pg. 36
13.	Crossword	Expert	Pg. 38
14.	Homophone Pairs	Advanced	Pg. 40
15.	Same But Different	Advanced	Pg. 47
16.	Sum It Up	Beginner	Pg. 48
17.	Collective Clues	Advanced	Pg. 53
18.	Word Attack	Expert	Pg. 54
19.	Spreading The Word	Advanced	Pg. 60
20.	Fortune Teller	Advanced	Pg. 62
21.	The Heat Is On	Beginner	Pg. 66
22.	Tongue Twisters	Beginner	Pg. 69
23.	Word Search II - Antonyms	Advanced	Pg. 70
24.	Sentence Charades	Advanced	Pg. 72
25.	Hidden Among The Trees	Beginner	Pg. 75
26.	Dial A Clue	Advanced	Pg. 76
27.	Scatter Platter	Advanced	Pg. 78
28.	Synonym Maze	Expert	Pg. 83

Contents

29.	Odd One Out	Advanced	Pg. 84
30.	Synonym Shake	Beginner	Pg. 86
31.	Being Instrumental	Beginner	Pg. 89
32.	Hang On Man	Advanced	Pg. 90
33.	Five Points	Advanced	Pg. 95
34.	Nonsense Poetry	Beginner	Pg. 97
35.	Hidden Link	Beginner	Pg. 98
36.	Kooky Cartoons	Beginner	Pg. 100
37.	Missing Word Sentences	Expert	Pg. 102
38.	Ridiculous Rhymes	Beginner	Pg. 104
39.	Story Builder	Beginner	Pg. 106
40.	Professionally Speaking	Beginner	Pg. 111
41.	Whale Of A Tale	Expert	Pg. 112
42.	Word Search III	Expert	Pg. 114
43.	Snap	Beginner	Pg. 116
44.	Anagrams	Expert	Pg. 123
45.	Square Roots	Advanced	Pg. 124
46.	Out Of Time	Expert	Pg. 130
47.	Idioms	Advanced	Pg. 133
48.	Best Fit	Advanced	Pg. 134
49.	Dot-to-Dot	Beginner	Pg. 136
50.	Missing Letter Antonyms	Expert	Pg. 138
51.	Antonym Maze	Expert	Pg. 139
52.	Tic Tac Toe	Expert	Pg. 140

Glossary   Pg. 144
Answer Key   Pg. 170

LEVEL: BEGINNER

Missing Link

Find the missing word that links of the other two words. These can be compound words or phrases. The first exercise has been done as an example.

1) cow _____boy_____ hood
2) light _____ boat
3) wash _____ mate
4) water _____ up
5) black _____ box
6) be _____ thought
7) waste _____ color
8) watch _____ over
9) suit _____ work
10) sheep _____ tight
11) head _____ maker
12) stage _____ shake
13) tail _____ way
14) come _____ town
15) turn _____ tail
16) wheel _____ man
17) star _____ bowl
18) turn _____ board
19) horse _____ trap
20) body _____ rail
21) duck _____ board
22) moth _____ park

WORD BANK

tower	skin
room	coat
chair	guard
house	line
fish	water
fly	ball
dress	key
bill	gate
boy	case
fore	hand
mail	down

| LEVEL: ADVANCED |

ANALOGIES

Use your growing vocabulary knowledge to match the analogies. The second pair of words will match in the same way as the first by picking from the choices given.

Example:
nib : pen   lens : frame / focus /(telescope)/ glass / stars

1. color : spectrum   waves : rock / beach / lap / sound / dolphin

2. angels : host   ship : flock / bunch / cast / tribe / flotilla

3. horse : equine   cat : mouse / bovine / piscine / elephantine / feline

4. seven : nine   twelve : eighteen / fourteen / ten / five / twenty

5. concur : disagree   dawdle : delay / draw / danger / rush / saunter

6. quay : key   raise : lift / above / rays / earn / wealth

7. tranquil : peaceful   stop : adopt / surprise / prohibit / accept / alter

8. impatient : patient   brisk : leisurely / brisket / quickly / definitely / wisely

9. methodical : organized   rupture : repair / hurt / break / mend / fix

10. diplomatic : tactful   lucid : clever / hard / clear / tricky / wide / loose

11. crucial : unnecessary   heavy : large / bulky / light / thick / burdensome

12. strife : peace   wide : long / fat / thick / narrow / sharp

13. chatter : talk   ballet : pirouette / tap / shoes / dance / leotard

14. burgundy : red   indigo : white / blue / orange / green / yellow

15. 10 : decade   1000 : year / century / millennium / thousand / time

16. bat : cave   bee : sting / swarm / honey / hive / nest

17. brass : cornet   string : pipe / tuba / harp / clarinet / drum

18. skyscraper : steel   igloo : house / cold / singing / snow / polar bear

19. sleet : precipitation   email : computer / text / letter / communication / laptop

20. single : solo   pair : duel / donut / duodenum / trio / duo

9

LEVEL: BEGINNER

You're Breaking Up

This section features words that have been broken up into pictures. This can help you remember some tricky words.

<u>Clue</u>

  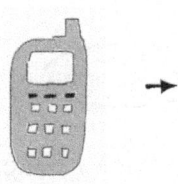 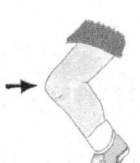 loud noise

 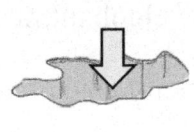  E furniture

 A  directory

in  U  vaccinate

 O 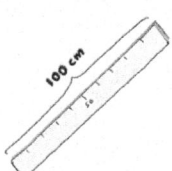 pressure

X  gone forever

10

You're Breaking Up

    material

    no re-print

    able to keep afloat

    in your head

    optimistic

Word Bank: barometer, buoyant, cacophony, catalog, copyright, extinct, inoculate, mentally, sanguine, textile, upholstery

LEVEL: ADVANCED

FAKE NEWS

Discover what really happened. Replace the underlined words in the sentences with the antonyms (opposites) from the list below:

OVERJOYED	PROGRESS	DECEITFUL
ENDANGERED	THWARTED	ORIGINAL
TIDY	DUSK	SUMMIT
LOYALTY	PARAMOUNT	ANXIOUS
PRAISED	SURPLUS	

1) The **replica** painting was stolen by the **honest** trickster.

2) The **safe** animals were **confident** on the journey home.

3) **Betrayal** was something the mayor valued.

4) Getting a new job was of **least** importance to Charles.

5) Tom's **unkempt** bedroom made his father **distraught**.

6) The snow **increased** the climbers chances of reaching the **nadir** of the mountain

7) The coach commended the player for the **regression** in his dribbling skills.

8) There was a **dearth** of fresh fruit at the farmer's market.

9) Toni **chastised** the man for saving her son's life.

10) Aubrey's parents told him to return home by **dawn**.

12

FAKE NEWS

Use the following words in the next ten sentences:

REALISTIC	STRATEGY	ENCOURAGED
LOFTY	FORMIDABLE	REINFORCED
EXPANSION	DECADE	EXAGGERATE
TOLERATE		

11) There was an **contraction** in the number of teams in the league.

12) Gerald hadn't seen his grandmother in over a **century**.

13) Sean had the **lowly** goal of attending a well-respected college.

14) Martha couldn't **reject** her sister's obnoxious behavior.

15) The store owner faced **feeble** competition from online retailers.

16) The General **weakened** his defenses by deploying more soldiers.

17) The coach had a unique **disorganization** for winning the game.

18) The children were **disheartened** by their progress in learning algebra.

19) It was **impractical** for Albert to think that studying would help improve his vocabulary.

20) Although he never got a top score, Stewart liked to **downplay** his talent at video games.

LEVEL: ADVANCED

WORD SEARCH I
SYNONYMS

First, find the <u>synonyms</u> of the words below by matching them with the words in the word bank. Next, look for the <u>synonyms</u> in the word search on the opposite page. Words may be in the puzzle forwards or backwards, diagonally or vertically.

                                                     SYNONYM

CHEAT   _____
PERSUADE   _____
NEXT TO   _____
GAIN   _____
A PRICE ESTIMATE   _____
UNIMPORTANT   _____
EXAMINE IN DETAIL   _____
UGLY   _____
COVER   _____
MORE IMPORTANT   _____
MAYHEM   _____
WELL BUILT   _____
MODEST   _____
TO SUPPLY WATER TO   _____
JOKER   _____
BLACK   _____
PEACEFUL   _____
LUXURIOUS   _____
STARTING POINT   _____
FIERCE   _____

WORD BANK

GROTESQUE	ORIGIN	LAVISH	CHAOS	BENEFIT	JESTER
FEROCIOUS	HUMBLE	COAX	EBONY	TRIVIAL	
SHROUD	SWINDLE	STURDY	QUOTE	TRANQUIL	
ADJACENT	IRRIGATE	ANALYZE	PRIORITY		

14

WORD SEARCH I
SYNONYMS

```
F R A L I R R I G A T E S Q
E C A D Y X W H U M B L E U
R A N P T M O D U O R H S T
O N A S I T R A N Q U I L I
C O L W R W B Y H O G I N F
I S Y A O D O S W I N D L E
O H Z D I B L E T U Q B U N
U R E J R V Q U O R F Q E E
S O L A P J I R E T S E J B
E W P C T N L R A E S H O L
T R A E I N S E T G R O T A
O N L N F O Y O R I G I N V
Q U O T E L R X A O C E G I
P G Q O N G U E S H L U R S
S T U R D Y N Q U E C P E H
```

15

LEVEL: ADVANCED

SNAKES AND LADDERS

Play the game in the traditional manner, with each player throwing the dice in turn, moving forward the corresponding number of squares along and up the board.

Usually landing on the bottom of the ladder means that you automatically move up to the top of it. Alternately if you land on a square with the snake's head you slip down to the square where the snake's tail ends.

In this version, before beginning, cut out the snake and ladder cards and place them in two piles. If you land at the bottom of a ladder, you must answer a ladder card first. To do this, you must provide an **antonym** for the word in capitals (a possible answer is provided on the back). If successful, then the player may climb to the top of the ladder. If they incorrectly answer, they must stay in the square they landed on, and will have to roll the dice to move on their next turn.

If you land on square with a snake's head, then you do not automatically slide down. You can save your position by correctly providing a **synonym** to the word given in capitals on one of the snake cards.

Note: You may have an equally good answer as the one on the back of the card. Use your good judgement to decide if it is indeed a good match. To win you must reach the 100 number square before any other player.

The game board, and cards are provided on the next pages. You can also create more cards using the words from the back of the book.

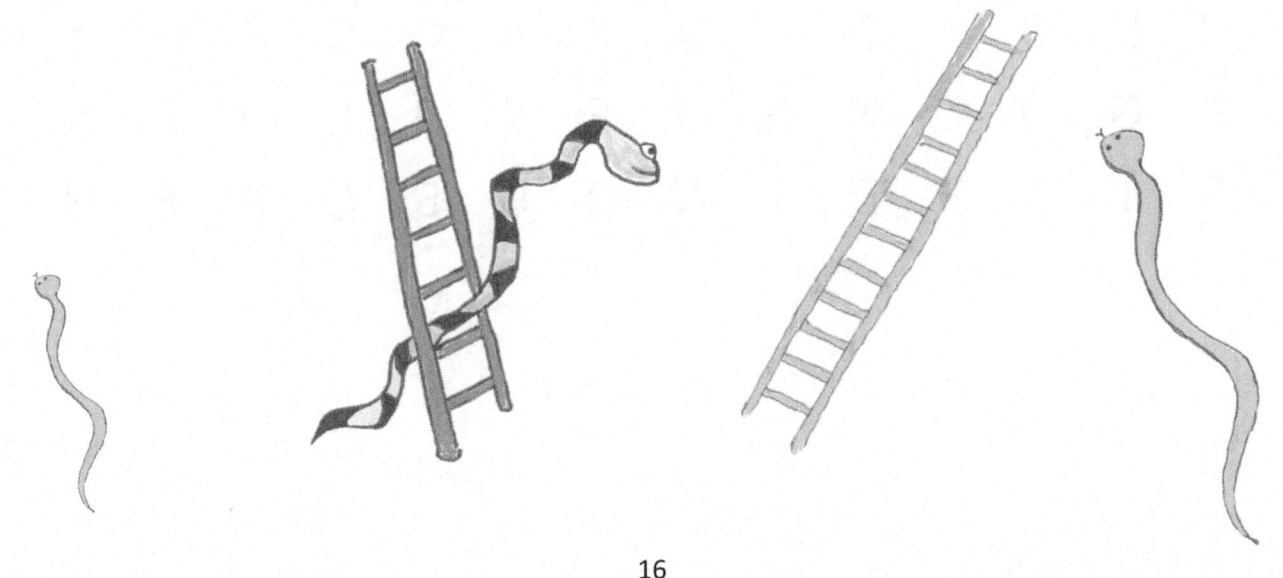

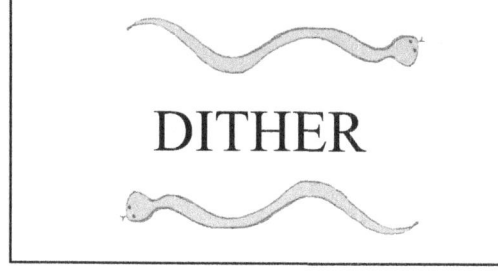
DITHER

MALADY

MALICIOUS

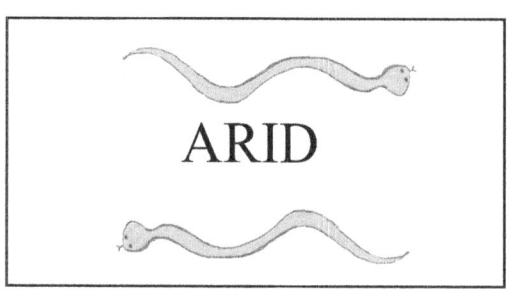
ARID

SABOTAGE

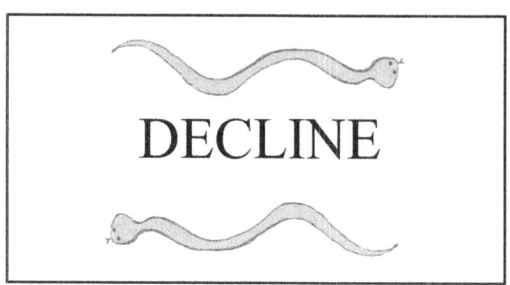
DECLINE

CHASTISE

PERISH

HAPLESS

CEASE

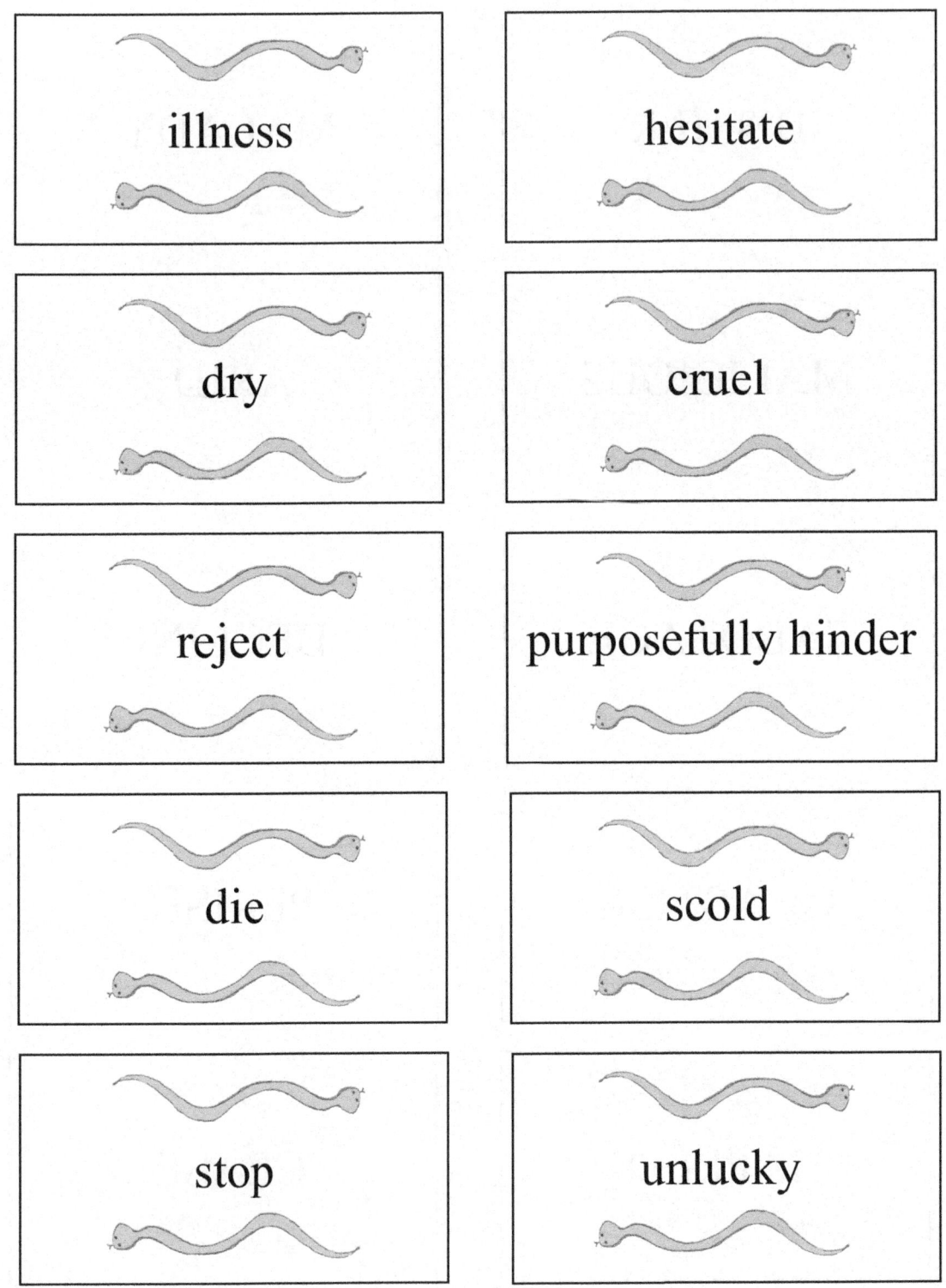

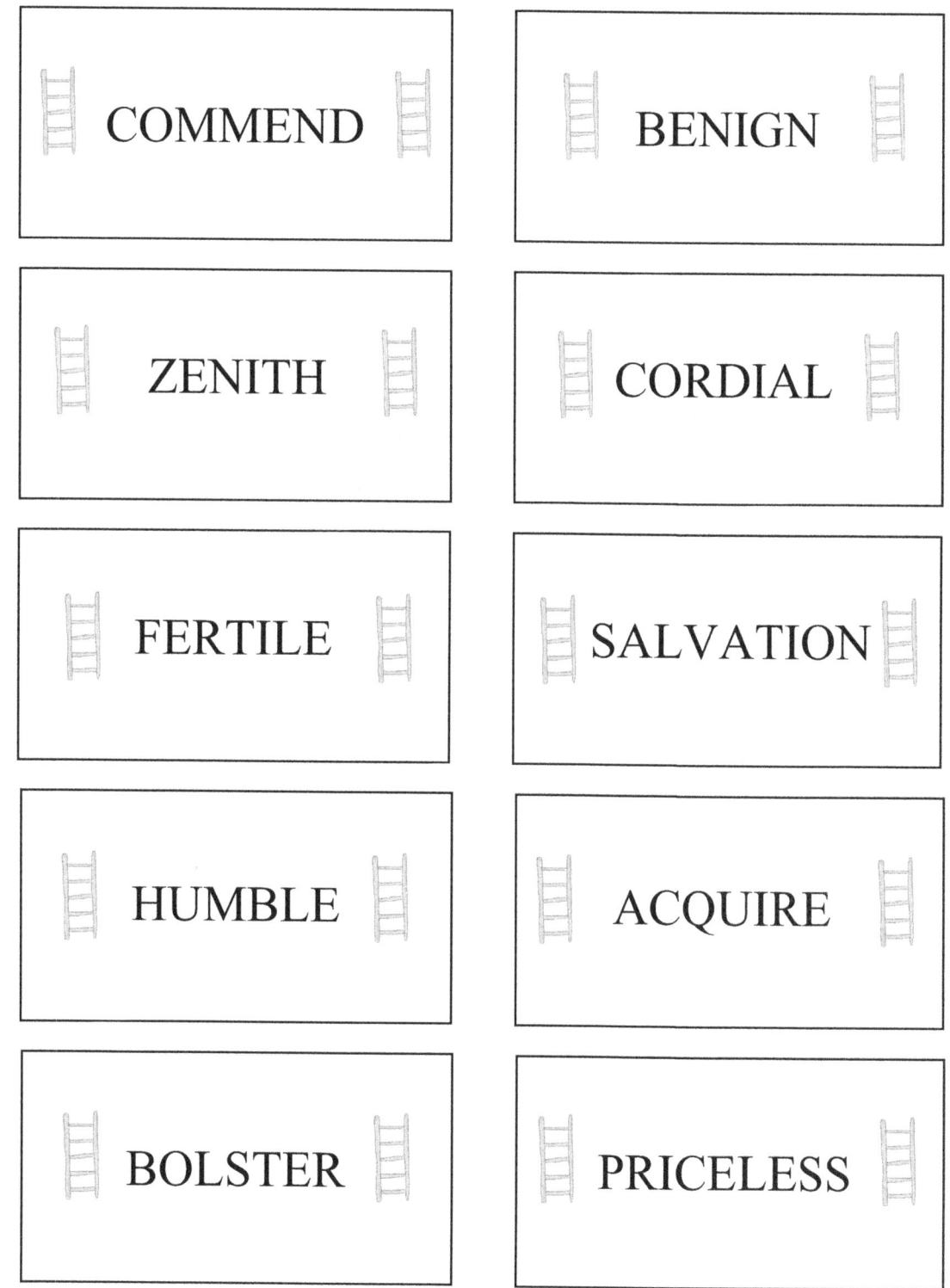

bad	insult
unfriendly	nadir
destruction	barren
lose	boastful
worthless	weaken

Snakes and Ladders Board

100 WIN	99	98	97	96	95	94	93	92	91
81	82	83	84	85	86	87	88	89	90
80	79	78	77	76	75	74	73	72	71
61	62	63	64	65	66	67	68	69	70
60	59	58	57	56	55	54	53	52	51
41	42	43	44	45	46	47	48	49	50
40	39	38	37	36	35	34	33	32	31
21	22	23	24	25	26	27	28	29	30
20	19	18	17	16	15	14	13	12	11
1 START	2	3	4	5	6	7	8	9	10

LEVEL: ADVANCED

SHOP 'TIL YOU DROP

Michelle's grandfather has given her a shopping list. Her problem is, she doesn't know where to buy the various items. Show her where to go to find each item. Write the item underneath the appropriate shop on the next page.

Can you think of any other items that might be available at these shops?

SHOPPING LIST

SHAWL	ENCYCLOPEDIA
TROUT	ARMOIRE
BASS	RHODODDENDRON
AUTOBIOGRAPHY	TRAMPOLINE
BEGONIA	CLEATS
RACQUET	CUFFLINKS
PEONY	TEXTILES
BROOCH	THIMBLE
REMNANTS	ANTHOLOGY
GOGGLES	BERET
BUREAU	LOCKET
FUTON	CRAVAT
GOWN	HADDOCK
SHIN PADS	SERIES
HUTCH	COD
DAISY	PATTERNS

LEVEL: EXPERT

SYNONYMS IN THE WILD

Read the passage below from Jack London's novel *White Fang* and use the context of the story to figure out the highlighted words. Use the list of synonyms at the end of the section to help.

****

The day began **auspiciously**. They had lost no dogs during the night, and they swung out upon the trail and into the silence, the darkness, and the cold with spirits that were fairly light. Bill seemed to have forgotten his **forebodings** of the previous night, and even waxed **facetious** with the dogs when, at midday, they overturned the sled on a bad piece of trail.

It was an **awkward** mix-up. The sled was upside down and jammed between a tree-trunk and a huge rock, and they were forced to unharness the dogs in order to straighten out the tangle. The two men were bent over the sled and trying to right it, when Henry observed One Ear sidling away.

"Here, you, One Ear!" he cried, straightening up and turning around on the dog.

But One Ear broke into a run across the snow, his traces trailing behind him. And there, out in the snow of their back track, was the she-wolf waiting for him. As he neared her, he became suddenly cautious. He slowed down to an alert and mincing walk and then stopped. He regarded her carefully and **dubiously**, yet desirefully. She seemed to smile at him, showing her teeth in an **ingratiating** rather than a **menacing** way. She moved toward him a few steps, playfully, and then halted. One Ear drew near to her, still alert and cautious, his tail and ears in the air, his head held high.

He tried to sniff noses with her, but she retreated playfully and coyly. Every advance on his part was accompanied by a **corresponding** retreat on her part. Step by step she was luring him away from the security of his human companionship. Once, as though a warning had in **vague** ways flitted through his intelligence, he turned his head and looked back at the overturned sled, at his team-mates, and at the two men who were calling to him.

SYNONYMS IN THE WILD

But whatever idea was forming in his mind, was **dissipated** by the she-wolf, who advanced upon him, sniffed noses with him for a fleeting instant, and then resumed her **coy** retreat before his renewed advances.

****

Match these synonyms with the highlighted words:

1. DOUBTFULLY, SUSPICIOUSLY _____

2. UNCLEAR _____

3. FAWNING, CHARMING _____

4. COMPARABLE, LIKE _____

5. FAVORABLY, PROMISING _____

6. JOKING, AMUSING _____

7. DIFFICULT, UNGRACEFUL _____

8. THREATENING, ALARMING _____

9. UNEASINESS, APPREHENSIONS _____

10. DISPELLED, SCATTERED _____

11. SHY _____

LEVEL: BEGINNER

WHERE AM I?

Find the **grid location** of these images hidden in the picture on the following pages, writing the grid numbers next to each word. Be careful, some of the pictures do not have a word!

HELIX	FLOTILLA
FOLIAGE	HYDRANT
FELINE	PEAK
PACHYDERM	FOUNDRY
REPTILE	BANNER
AMPHIBIAN	CREEK
TAMBOURINE	HADDOCK
MANOR	IMP
DINGHY	TEAL
MACE	SOMBRERO
BOVINE	CANINE
STALLION	FORTRESS

BONUS: Can you find the **dromedary**?

A4	A5	A6
B4	B5	B6
C4	C5	C6

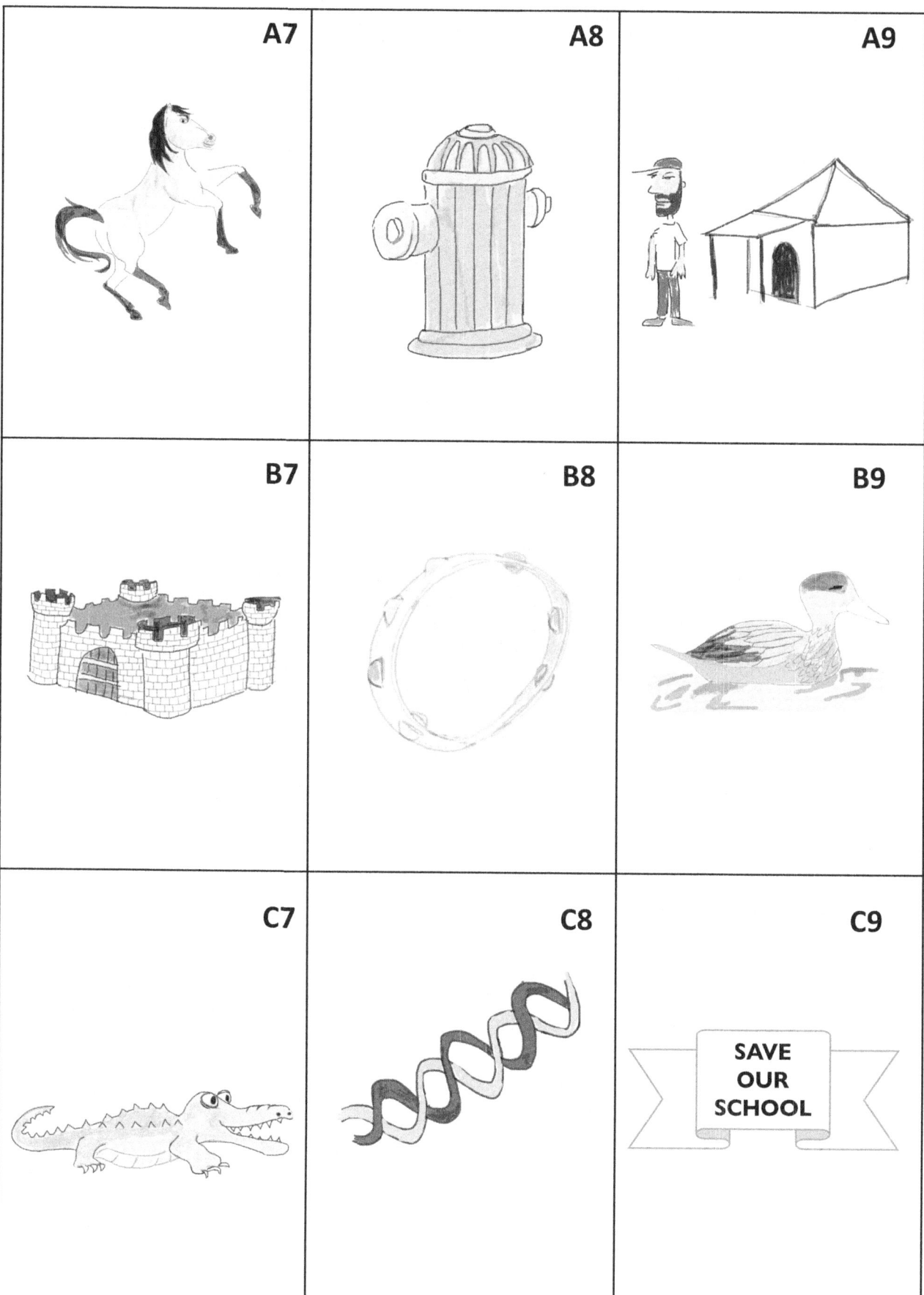

LEVEL: ADVANCED

FUNNY FACES

Pictures can be useful in helping to remember vocabulary and also stimulate discussion about synonyms.

In this example:

Appropriate answers could range from -

- Happy   - Excited
- Overjoyed   - Thrilled
- Delighted   - Pleased
- Radiant   - Buoyant

Cut out the cards on the following pages and try to identify the emotion or idea being expressed. Possible answers will be on the back of each card.

What other synonyms can match these words? See if you can think of at least TWO adjectives to describe the picture.

Can you create more cards using your own drawings?

ludicrous childish, ridiculous, silly	**irate** furious, upset, angry
jovial friendly, festive	**affluent** rich, wealthy
bilingual interpreter, translator	**feeble** weak, frail, puny
exasperated agitated, annoyed	**nimble** agile, quick
despondent dejected, depressed	**valiant** gallant, courageous

affable amiable, cheerful	**bashful** shy, self-conscious
vain conceited, arrogant	**haughty** snobby, snooty
malicious hateful, vicious	**industrious** hard-working, diligent
perplexed bewildered, puzzled	**indolent** lazy, lethargic
deceitful deceptive, misleading	**prodigy** gifted, genius

FILL _ IN _ THE _ BLANKS

LEVEL: EXPERT

Find the missing letters that completes the first word, but also the second word on the right. The first two exercises have been done as an example. Do you know the meaning of both words?

    stop open   cape peak

1) ST <u>O P</u> EN   2) CA <u>P E</u> AK

3) FL <u>E D</u> IT   4) EA <u>C H</u> ILL

5) SO <u>F A</u> CT   6) TA <u>M E</u> ND

7) TR <u>O P E</u> N   8) LAUN <u>C H</u> IDE

9) SP <u>U R</u> GE   10) GAUNT <u>L E T</u> TER

11) CIV <u>I L</u> LEGAL   12) BAL <u>M Y</u> RIAD

13) AFFLU <u>E N T</u> RANCE   14) CONST <u>A N T</u> AGONIZE

15) NIM <u>B L E</u> NDER   16) PRINCI <u>P A L</u> INDROME

17) AUSPICI <u>O U S</u> TED   18) DISO <u>B E Y</u> OND

19) CHAPER <u>O N E</u> ROUS   20) ECONOMI <u>C A L</u> LOUS

35

LEVEL: BEGINNER

Word Ladders

Word Ladders change one word into another by altering <u>one</u> letter per each step, creating a new word on each rung as you go **down** the ladder. The first exercise has been done as an example.

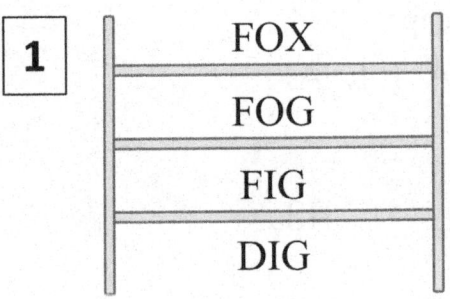

1. FOX / FOG / FIG / DIG

Clues:
a. mist
b. a soft, pear-shaped fruit

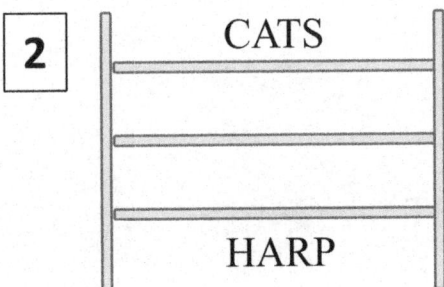

2. CATS / ___ / ___ / HARP

Clues:
a. automobiles
b. type of fish

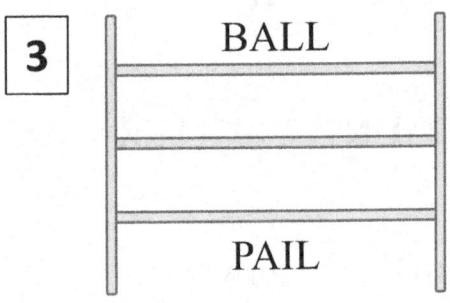

3. BALL / ___ / ___ / PAIL

Clues:
a. decrease
b. unsuccessful

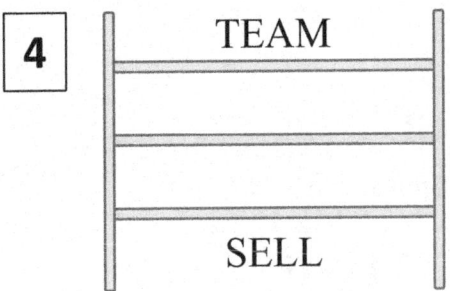

4. TEAM / ___ / ___ / SELL

Clues:
a. color or a type of duck
b. to say

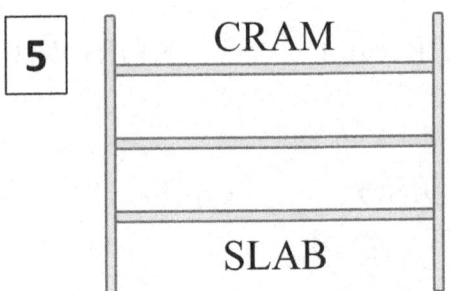

5. CRAM / ___ / ___ / SLAB

Clues:
a. type of mollusk
b. shut forcefully

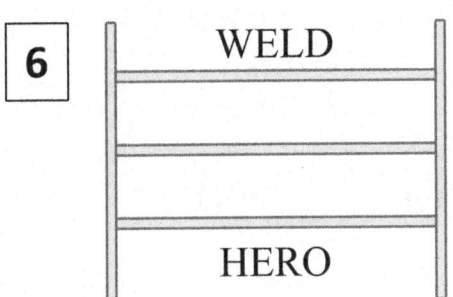

6. WELD / ___ / ___ / HERO

Clues:
a. grasped
b. group of animals

Word Ladders

7 WORM → TART

Clues:
a. shape
b. place for some animals
c. damage
d. male deer
e. wagon

8 CLAP → SHOP

Clues:
a. prune, shear
b. lose one's footing
c. small incision
d. groove
e. an attempt

9 SCORE → SMART

Clues:
a. biscuit-like cake
b. rock
c. depot
d. gaze
e. commence

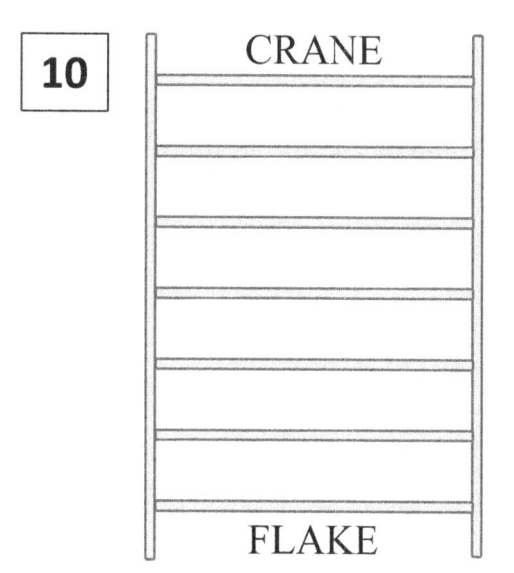

10 CRANE → FLAKE

Clues:
a. desire greatly
b. extremely serious
c. clearing
d. knife edge
e. accusation
f. blaze

LEVEL: EXPERT

CROSSWORD

A crossword puzzle can be a great way to reinforce the use of words and spelling. If you need to, use the word bank at the bottom of the page to help you complete the puzzle.

ACCROSS

1) Second to last
6) A reflected sound that comes back to the listener
8) Foul, spoiled
10) Mild, kind, not strong
12) A symbol
14) A difficult situation
16) Homophone for two
17) A specific day on the calendar
18) A purpose or intention
20) Devoured
22) To prevent someone from getting something
25) A way out
27) To throw
29) To arrive at
30) A trick or deception
31) To spoil, harm the appearance of something
33) To participate in an election
35) Anger
36) Vegetable found in a pod
38) Very brave, heroic
39) Consuming
41) Strained; taut or rigid
42) Necessity
43) Affirmative
44) To choose to take up or follow

DOWN

1) To allow
2) Negative
3) Not certain
4) A list of things to be done
5) Respect, admiration
7) A natural home or environment
9) Showing kindness, gentleness
11) Not complicated
13) To conceal
15) To compete for something
19) Casually calm and relaxed
21) To leave one's own country and settle permanently in another
23) To dig up
24) To walk around arrogantly, trying to look important
26) Being economical, using money wisely
27) Regrets or is disappointed
28) A bovine animal
31) Lacking in quantity
32) Overt, obvious
34) Chicks come from these
37) Opposite direction to West
40) To move your head in agreement

WORD BANK: adopt, adversity, agenda, aim, ate, cover, date, deprive, east, easy, eating, echo, egg, emigrate, esteem, excavate, exit, gallant, gentle, habitat, hoax, icon, ire, laments, lob, mar, meager, need, nod, nonchalant, not, open, ox, pea, penultimate, permit, reach, rotten, strut, tender, tense, tentative, thrifty, to, vie, vote, yes

CROSSWORD

LEVEL: ADVANCED

HOMOPHONE PAIRS

A homophone is a word that is pronounced the same as another word, but has a different meaning.

The cards on the following pages make sets of homophone pairs. After cutting out the cards, spread them out over your table. Take it in turns to lift two cards. If they ARE homophone pairs AND you can define both meanings, you keep the pair. If they are not homophone pairs, return them to the table and the next player has a turn.

The winner collects the most pairs.

Do not feel that you need to use all of the cards in every game. Twenty new words to learn in a week is plenty. If you do not know the meanings, look in the glossary at the back of the book.

Example:

Loot = money and valuables, often stolen

Lute = a pear-shaped, string instrument

pairs	pears
leak	leek
rays	raise
lax	lacks
hoarse	horse
axes	axis
guise	guys
base	bass
foul	fowl
based	baste

homophone pairs	homophone pairs
homophone pairs	homophone pairs
homophone pairs	homophone pairs
homophone pairs	homophone pairs
homophone pairs	homophone pairs
homophone pairs	homophone pairs
homophone pairs	homophone pairs
homophone pairs	homophone pairs
homophone pairs	homophone pairs
homophone pairs	homophone pairs

dense	dents
chord	cord
cent	scent
callous	callus
boar	bore
bald	bawled
ewes	yews
genes	jeans
real	reel
need	knead

homophone pairs	homophone pairs
homophone pairs	homophone pairs
homophone pairs	homophone pairs
homophone pairs	homophone pairs
homophone pairs	homophone pairs
homophone pairs	homophone pairs
homophone pairs	homophone pairs
homophone pairs	homophone pairs
homophone pairs	homophone pairs
homophone pairs	homophone pairs

morning	mourning
gait	gate
beach	beech
shoot	chute
principle	principal
waive	wave
yoke	yolk
symbol	cymbal
rye	wry
role	roll

homophone pairs	homophone pairs
homophone pairs	homophone pairs
homophone pairs	homophone pairs
homophone pairs	homophone pairs
homophone pairs	homophone pairs
homophone pairs	homophone pairs
homophone pairs	homophone pairs
homophone pairs	homophone pairs
homophone pairs	homophone pairs
homophone pairs	homophone pairs

LEVEL: ADVANCED

Same But Different

Heteronyms are words that are spelled the same, but pronounced differently and have different meanings. Can you find the words below? The first one has been done as an example

	Clue	*Answer*
1.	be pleased / what's included	content
2.	to rip / waterdrop coming from the eye	_____
3.	garbage / to decline	_____
4.	nearby / to shut	_____
5.	not true / someone very ill	_____
6.	to disagree / a thing	_____
7.	a document giving permission / to allow	_____
8.	to injure / coiled up	_____
9.	a summary of work experience / to start again	_____
10.	to comfort / an upright case	_____
11.	to shine / something from Poland	_____
12.	to introduce / a gift	_____
13.	to let someone off / an explanation	_____
14.	to argue about something / a game	_____
15.	to make / vegetables	_____

47

LEVEL: BEGINNER

Sum It Up

The object of this game is to create words by combining two cards.

| in | -side |

Cut out the cards, and shuffle them. Each player takes two cards – do not show your cards to the other player(s). All of the other cards should go into a pile face down.

Players take turns drawing a new card.

If a player draws a card and cannot create a word, they should place one of their cards back under the pile. Then the next player takes a turn.

If the player draws a card that can be combined with one of their other cards to create a word, then the player gets a point and sets those cards aside. They should then draw one more card, and let the next player take a turn.

The player with the most completed words wins.

am	-bush
ab	-stain
am	-icable
en	-dure
en	-danger
ab	-olish
ab	-sent
as	-pect
as	-pire
in	-ferno

Sum It Up	Sum It Up
Sum It Up	Sum It Up
Sum It Up	Sum It Up
Sum It Up	Sum It Up
Sum It Up	Sum It Up
Sum It Up	Sum It Up
Sum It Up	Sum It Up
Sum It Up	Sum It Up
Sum It Up	Sum It Up
Sum It Up	Sum It Up

am	-phibian
in	-dulge
car	-go
car	-bon
in	-scribe
am	-ulet
in	-sure
as	-cend

Sum It Up	Sum It Up
Sum It Up	Sum It Up
Sum It Up	Sum It Up
Sum It Up	Sum It Up
Sum It Up	Sum It Up
Sum It Up	Sum It Up
Sum It Up	Sum It Up
Sum It Up	Sum It Up

LEVEL: ADVANCED

COLLECTIVE CLUES

Find the collective term or expression. The first example has been given.

CLUE   COLLECTIVE NOUNS

Ground Defenders   __**army**__ of ants

Fill your suitcase   _____ of wolves

A great feeling   _____ of lions

Peas live here   _____ of whales

Put it in the trash can   _____ of puppies

To kill someone   _____ of crows

Bird's home   _____ of vipers

TV programme leader   _____ of angels

Grey rock used for roof tiles   _____ of candidates

String, wind, brass and percussion form this   _____ of crickets

An explosive collection   _____ of guns

Beer is often carried in this   _____ of laughs

Shake a little   _____ of arrows

Somewhere to sleep   _____ of oysters

Swim here   _____ of typists

It makes me itchy thinking about a   _____ of mosquitoes

First finger   _____ of names

Grab hold!   _____ of eggs

53

LEVEL: EXPERT

WORD ATTACK

This is a two-player game. The objective of the game is to sink the other player's ships, before they can sink yours! Spend some time learning the word meanings for two of the word sets (opposite) before beginning the game. For example, use sets A and B in the first week.

Setup: Each player receives a game board page. Cut out the 5 game pieces and lay them on the MY SHIPS grid (Alternately, draw in the ships on your paper). The ships must be placed either horizontally or vertically, as shown in the picture. Do not allow your opponent to see where you have placed your ships!

Each player should also get a list of words.

Gameplay: Players take turns making guesses as to where their opponent's ships might be, using grid coordinates. Guesses should be recorded in the MY GUESSES grid so that players have a complete record and don't guess the same space twice.

Before taking a turn, a player must give a correct definition or synonym to one of the words from their opponent's word list. If they answer incorrectly, then they miss the chance to guess a coordinate.

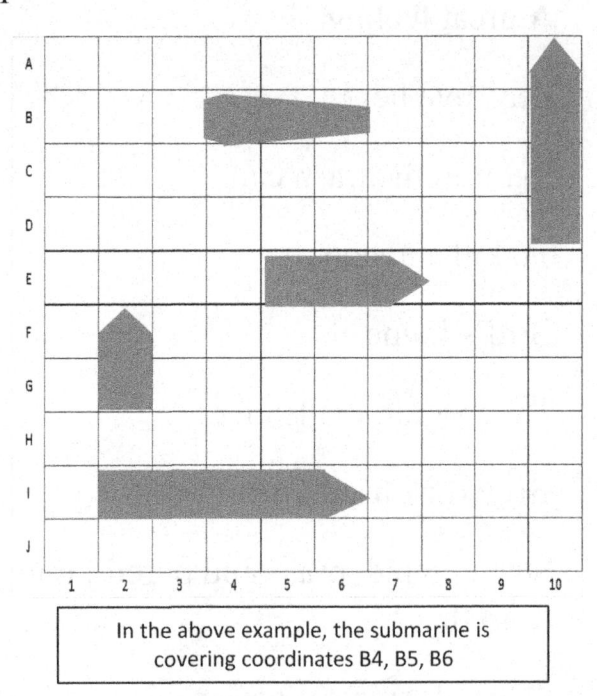

In the above example, the submarine is covering coordinates B4, B5, B6

Once all of the words on a list have been used, start again with the same list. This will help reinforce comprehension.

When a player guesses a grid space, for example D-10, the other player must say either "HIT" or "MISS," depending on whether their ship is placed in that grid. In the example above, it would be a "HIT." When all spaces the ship is covering have been guessed by the opponent, the player should announce that their ship has been sunk by saying, "You sunk my ship!"

The game ends when one of the players has lost all of their ships.

Note: This game can be played many times using the different sets of battle words, or you can make additional lists using words from the glossary.

ATTACK WORDS

SET A	SET B
INDUSTRIOUS	TEPEE
DEMOLISH	ESCALATE
DEVIOUS	LIVID
GOWN	SEVERE
OASIS	COPIOUS
RESOLVE	URN
CONTEMPORARY	AFFILIATION
COMPASS	CONDEMN
ABUNDANCE	CONDIMENT
PALINDROME	EXPENDITURE

SET C	SET D
STRUT	GRUESOME
MAIZE	BURDEN
TORSO	FUTILE
FLAWLESS	UMPIRE
IMPEDE	FATHOM
FORGO	COARSE
ABHORRENT	MIRTH
VERTEBRATE	LIABLE
YOLK	GAVEL
MAIM	NAUSEOUS

ATTACK WORDS

SET E

INFLUENCE
FERMENT
VILLAIN
JEER
DILUTE
AMPHIBIAN
ACCURATE
PLACID
DEARTH
FABRICATION

SET F

OPTIMISTIC
DIRE
DEMEANOR
CROCHET
CATASTROPHE
AID
CHAPERONE
FALTER
OPAQUE
APPALLED

SET G

TEMPLATE
UNANIMOUS
GAUNTLET
TENTATIVE
NOVICE
DISSIPATE
NONENTITY
CLARIFY
PRECIPITATION
REBUKE

SET H

POSTPONE
PUNGENT
BESIEGED
TABLET
FOLIAGE
THEATER
AMASS
GARGANTUAN
BLACKLIST
PULSATE

Word Attack Game Pieces

Player 1

Agile Aircraft Carrier (5 spaces)

Lethal Large ship (4 spaces)

Deceptive Destroyer (3 spaces)

Swift Submarine (3 spaces)

Perilous Patrol Boat (2 spaces)

Player 2

Agile Aircraft Carrier (5 spaces)

Lethal Large ship (4 spaces)

Deceptive Destroyer (3 spaces)

Swift Submarine (3 spaces)

Perilous Patrol Boat (2 spaces)

My Ships

My Guesses

My Ships

My Guesses

LEVEL: ADVANCED

S P R E A D I N G
T H E   W O R D

This is a technique that helps to reinforce words by giving a clue, and then challenging you to find the answer hidden between two different words.

Examples:

A healthy drink   car**ton** **ic**on = tonic

Material used for surfacing roads   gui**tar** **mac**aroni = tarmac

Severe physical or mental suffering   distribu**tor** **ment**al = torment

Clue: Find:

1. lively   wasp   rye

2. a living place   plod   gentle

3. get rid of   you   street

4. work hard   into   illegal

5. not very often   counsel   dome

6. get bigger   reflex   panda

7. someone that dies for a cause   grammar   tyranny

8. the very top   sum   mitten

9. joker   cow   itinerary

10. leave out   room   item

11. neither warm nor cold   step   idea

S P R E A D I N G   T H E   W O R D

12. bring into a country   shrimp   orthodontist
13. a promise   boa   three
14. arm or leg   slim   breach
15. to set light to   kind   lent
16. fake, not genuine   rash   amiable
17. big, enormous   lava   stream
18. to put completely into water   simmer   send
19. a loud noise   bend   include
20. a disease or illness   grandma   lady
21. clever   last   utensil
22. make a pained face   pilgrim   acetone
23. successor, next in line   tithe   irregular
24. something given   hairdo   national
25. a group of notes sounded together   anchor destiny
26. chemical element, fluorescent lighting insane onward
27. not active   eyelid   lethargic
28. of good behavior and principle tremor   almost
29. keeps a boat from moving   man   choral
30. give someone the story   abide   briefly
31. staunch, unyielding   homestead   fastidious
32. not gregarious   mimic   oyster

| LEVEL: ADVANCED |

FORTUNE TELLER

This is a game you might have played in school before, but now it can be used to help learn new words. First, find the definition of each word. Use the glossary to make sure you are learning the correct definitions before you practice.

Cut and fold the opposite page as you would for a fortune teller game:

- Lay the paper with the printed side facing down on the table and fold the four corners into the center
- Flip over and fold the four corners along the lines into the middle
- Fold over and back (one at a time) on the diagonal, vertical and horizontal lines to make the fortune teller flexible
- Place fingers underneath the flaps to hold the completed model (as shown below)

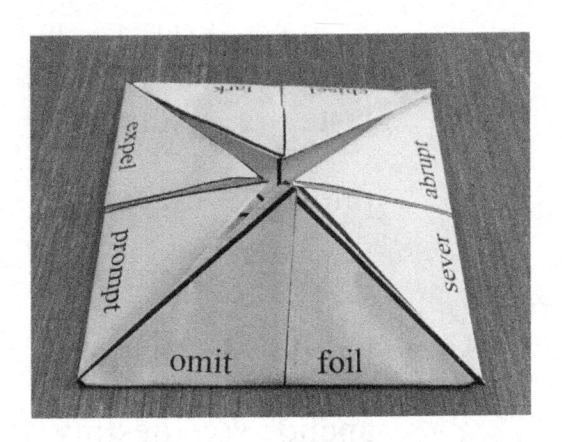

Step One – folded corners

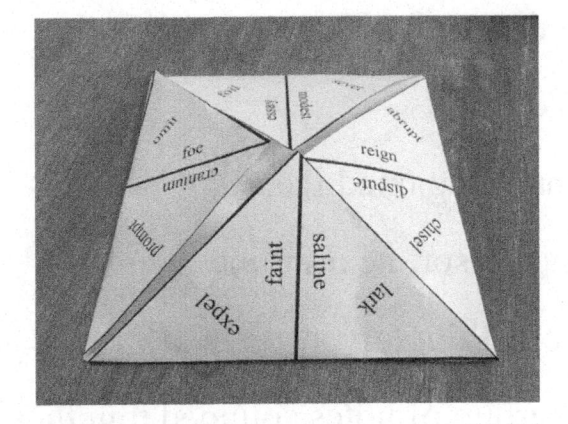

Step Two – folded corners

Completed model after folding along lines and fingers placed

FORTUNE TELLER

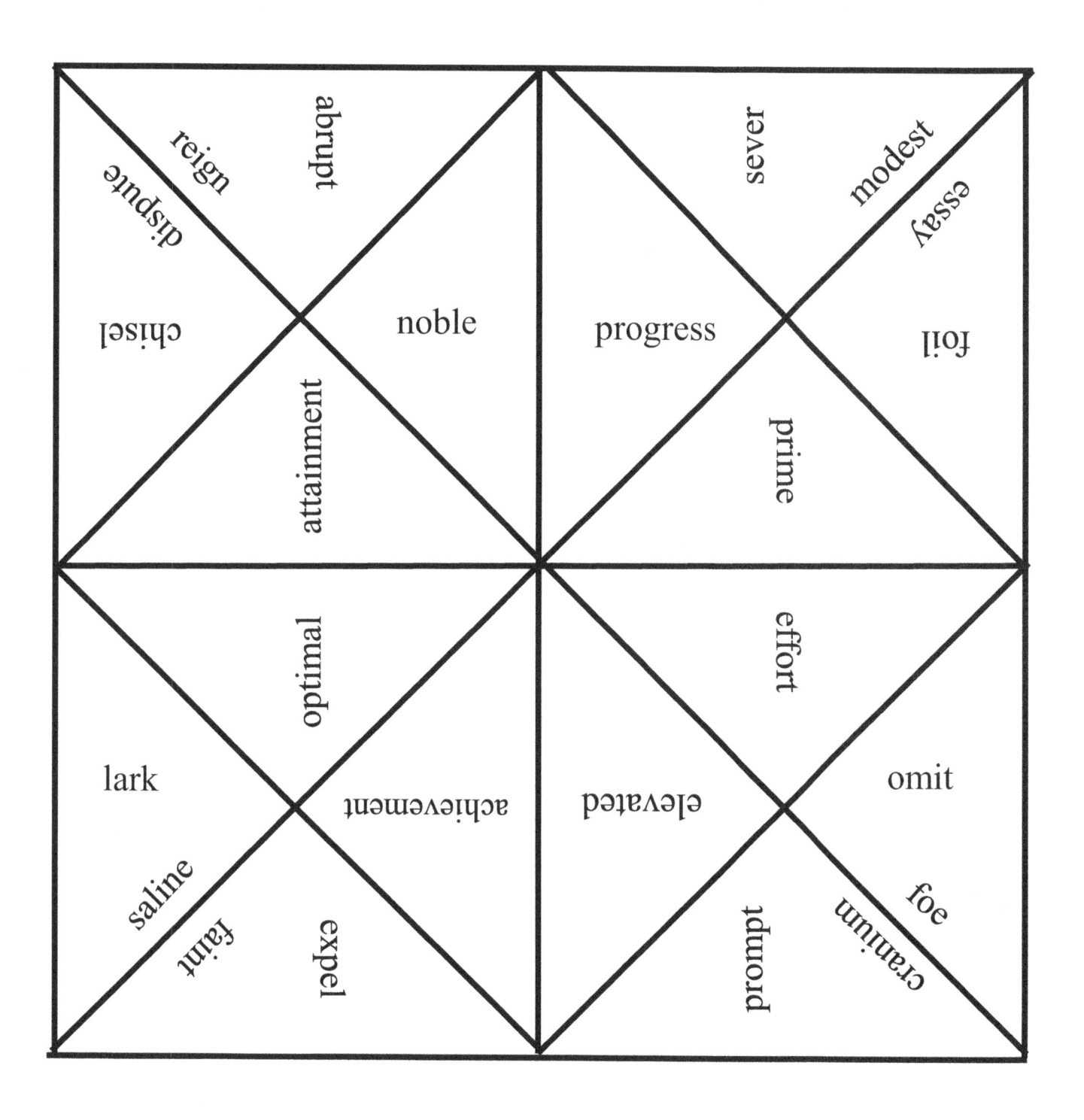

dispute	abrupt	sever	essay
reign			modest
chisel	noble	progress	foil
	attainment	prime	
	optimal	effort	
lark			omit
saline	achievement	elevated	foe
faint	expel	prompt	cranium

63

FORTUNE TELLER

This page left intentionally blank

FORTUNE TELLER

How to Play: This game is intended as a tactile way to practice words. Play in the traditional manner, however you may only move fingers if you can give a definition of your chosen word.

Start with the fortune teller closed and pick one of the words showing on the outside. Move fingers in and out the number of times that matches the number of letters in the word. Use the words on the inside until you have completed three turns correctly, and then you may open one of the inside flaps to find a new word (or fortune).

LEVEL: BEGINNER

THE HEAT IS ON!

The weather station forecasts that the temperature will rise! Cut out the words on the opposite page and discuss where they should go on the thermometer:

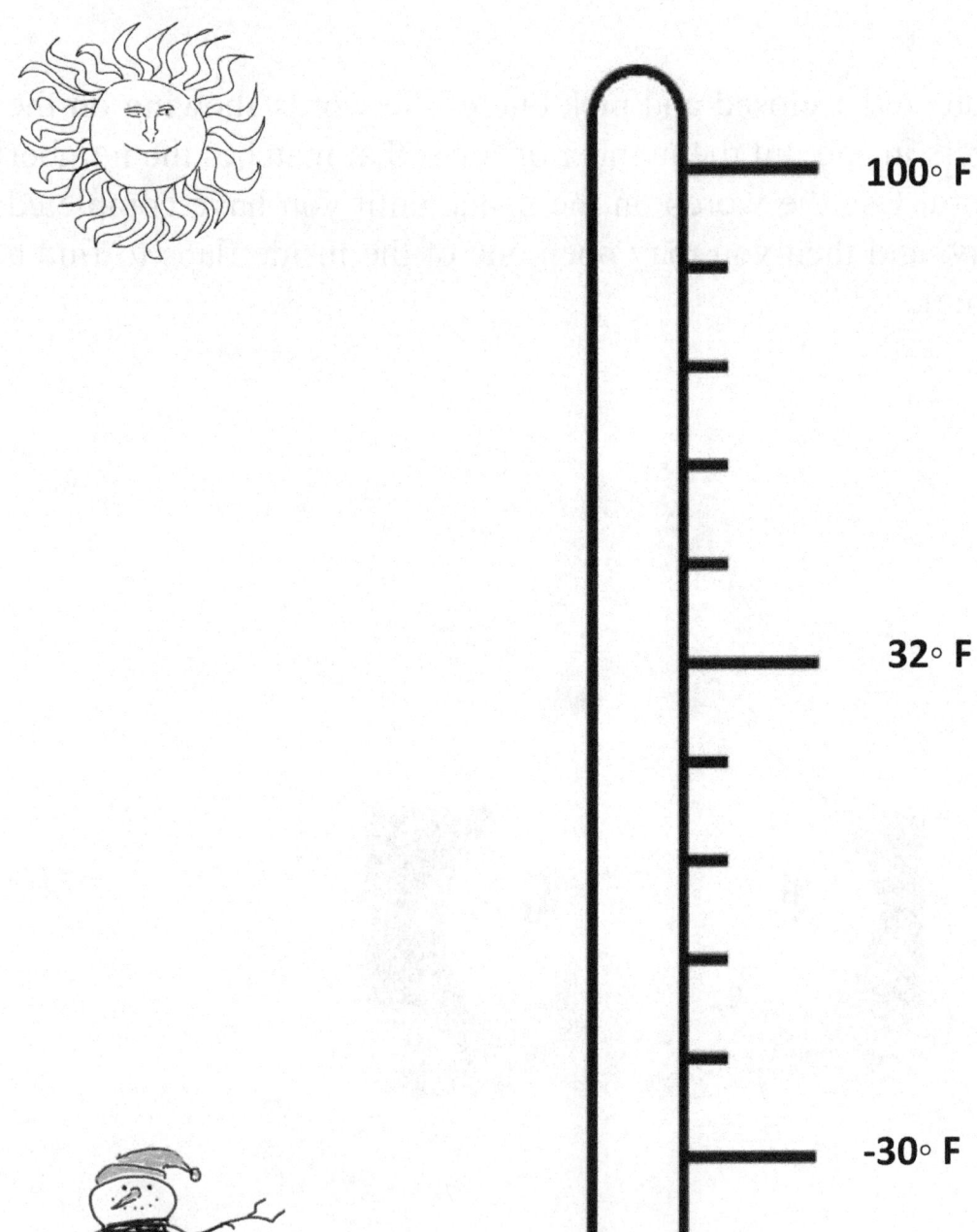

100° F

32° F

-30° F

biting	frosty	tropical
temperate	inclement	baking
balmy	sweltering	searing
tepid	chilly	frigid
lukewarm	scorching	icy
sultry	raw	freezing
sizzling	mild	humid

☀	☀	☀
☀	☀	☀
☀	☀	☀
☀	☀	☀
☀	☀	☀
☀	☀	☀
☀	☀	☀

LEVEL: BEGINNER

Tongue Twisters

Try and memorize these tongue twisters and say them as fast as you can!

1. DANGEROUS DAN DELETED DIGITAL DETAILS DILIGENTLY.

2. SQUEAMISH SQUIRRELS SQUEAL AND SQUABBLE.

3. KNOW-IT-ALL NOAH NEVER KNEW A NEATER NOVEL.

4. CUNNING KATIE CAUGHT CLAUDE CLIMBING CLIFFS.

5. PETER PESTERED PENELOPE TO PICK A PROPER PACKET.

6. ON MOST MONDAYS, MAX, MOLLY AND MANDY MINGLE.

7. RELIABLE REILLY RECTIFIED ROBBY'S ROTTEN WRITING.

8. IRATE IDA IRRITATED IRIS INCESSANTLY.

9. LOUD LARRY LIES LUCIDLY.

10. HOARDING HILDA HID HER HEAVY HULA HOOP IN HONOLULU.

11. PETER PERPETUATES PERFECT PROFESSIONAL PUNS.

12. TINA'S TINY TARDY TURTLES TRAIN IN TRANQUILTY.

LEVEL: ADVANCED

WORD SEARCH II
ANTONYMS

First, find the <u>antonyms</u> of the words below by matching them with the words in the word bank. Next, look for the <u>antonyms</u> in the word search on the opposite page. Words may be in the puzzle forwards or backwards, diagonally or vertically.

COMMON　　　　　＿＿＿＿＿＿＿＿＿＿

VERTICAL　　　　 ＿＿＿＿＿＿＿＿＿＿

UNMANAGEABLE　＿＿＿＿＿＿＿＿＿＿

BOLSTER　　　　　＿＿＿＿＿＿＿＿＿＿

MILD　　　　　　　＿＿＿＿＿＿＿＿＿＿

DIFFERENT　　　　＿＿＿＿＿＿＿＿＿＿

LOSE　　　　　　　＿＿＿＿＿＿＿＿＿＿

TINY　　　　　　　＿＿＿＿＿＿＿＿＿＿

PEACEFUL　　　　 ＿＿＿＿＿＿＿＿＿＿

SOAKED　　　　　＿＿＿＿＿＿＿＿＿＿

CONFRONT　　　　＿＿＿＿＿＿＿＿＿＿

ESTABLISH　　　　＿＿＿＿＿＿＿＿＿＿

VAGUE　　　　　　＿＿＿＿＿＿＿＿＿＿

ALERT　　　　　　 ＿＿＿＿＿＿＿＿＿＿

COWARDLY　　　　＿＿＿＿＿＿＿＿＿＿

HARMONY　　　　 ＿＿＿＿＿＿＿＿＿＿

UNKNOWN　　　　 ＿＿＿＿＿＿＿＿＿＿

DISCOURAGE　　　＿＿＿＿＿＿＿＿＿＿

FAKE　　　　　　　＿＿＿＿＿＿＿＿＿＿

INCLUDE　　　　　＿＿＿＿＿＿＿＿＿＿

WORD BANK

HEROIC	FAMILIAR	ACQUIRE	AVOID	ACCURATE
GENUINE	HORIZONTAL	ARID	SIMILAR	DROWSY
OBEDIENT	BELLIGERENT	MASSIVE	TENSION	PERSUADE
ABOLISH	OBSCURE	OMIT	EXHAUST	DRASTIC

WORD SEARCH II
ANTONYMS

```
O D I B A S R A L I M I S Y
I B E L H E O M L R H N A B
R W E K A E N O I S N E T
A S O D R R R M U N I S I N
I Y N O I S G O C S L M O I
L A S U D E L B I C O F C U
I C Q W Q O N N T C B T R Q
M C U I O U Y T S U A H X E
A U L O B R I F A V O I D V
F R K G S U D R R D I O U I
L A F A C M I L D R E A C S
G T S A U E D A U S R E P S
N E H O R I Z O N T A L B A
E T N G E N U I N E M N U M
B E L L I G E R E N T S A O
```

LEVEL: ADVANCED

SENTENCE CHARADES

Charades is a popular game for two or more players. Normally players act out clues to popular shows, books or movies. Here we are using it to reinforce key vocabulary.

Be sure you know the meanings of the following words::

IGNITED = lit
GINGERLY = carefully
FURIOUS = angry
CHERISHED = cared for
GEM = jewel
EXQUISITE = extremely beautiful
ASCENDED = went up
CAPTIVE = prisoner

MEANDERS = bends
UNPALATABLE = bad tasting
TALONS = large claws (bird)
SERENADE = sing romantically
PHOBIA = fear
CEASE = to stop
INFLEXIBLE = rigid

Players will have ONE MINUTE to look at all of the cards. Cards should then be cut out and placed face-down in a pile.

Players take turns to lift a card from the pile, and then act out a sentence. Other players attempt to guess the sentence. You can create more cards using words from the glossary in the back of the book.

Charade Sentence Cards

I ignited the fire gingerly but there was a furious blaze.	I cherished the glistening gem as it was exquisite.
The judge was inflexible and wouldn't free the captive.	The dog ascended the stairs
The river meanders for many miles.	The cook found the cake unpalatable.
The boyfriend serenaded his girlfriend just for fun.	Eagles have enormous talons.
The cat had a phobia regarding spiders.	When the clock strikes twelve, cease work!

CHARADES	CHARADES
CHARADES	CHARADES
CHARADES	CHARADES
CHARADES	CHARADES
CHARADES	CHARADES

LEVEL: BEGINNER

HIDDEN AMONG THE TREES

Find the 20 nouns that are types of trees.

Poinsettia
Barrel
Pitcher
Beech
Aspen
Walnut
Spruce
Poplar
Apple
Castle
Larder
Lion
Cleaver
Ash
Willow
Lance
Oak
Yew
Cherry
Birch
Juniper
Orchid
Vat
Dogwood
Pine
Fir
Magnolia
Barber
Maple
Rumor
Root
Plunder
Mansion
Elm
Bumble
Hickory

75

LEVEL: ADVANCED

Dial a Clue

Use the clue and the code (number) to work out the mystery words (synonym). You can look at these examples to see if there is a pattern:

CLUE	CODE	MYSTERY WORD
ONLY	6 3 7 3	MERE
CENTER	4 8 2	HUB

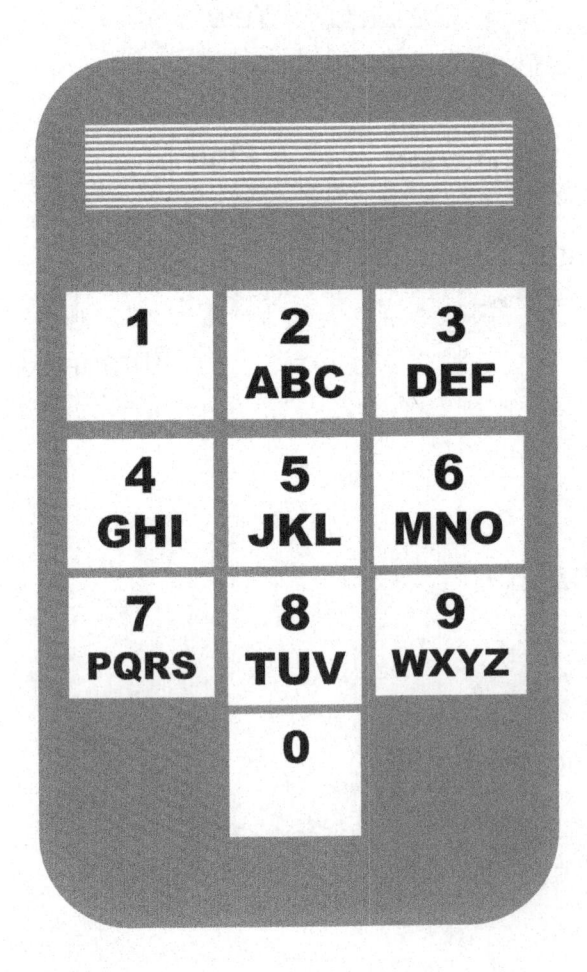

"May I have a clue, please."

Dial a Clue

CLUE	CODE	MYSTERY WORD
DONATE	4 4 8 3	_____
DEBATE	8 2 5 5	_____
INTERVAL	2 7 3 2 5	_____
AJAR	6 7 3 6	_____
SCRUFFY	7 4 2 2 2 9	_____
CONTEMPORARY	6 6 3 3 7 6	_____
DELAYED	5 2 8 3	_____
SKETCH	3 7 2 9	_____
FRET	9 6 7 7 9	_____
LABYRINTH	6 2 9 4	_____
AGILE	6 4 6 2 5 3	_____
AVOID	7 4 8 6	_____
FOUNDATION	2 2 7 3	_____
SUBSEQUENT	6 3 9 8	_____
CRUEL	8 6 5 4 6 3	_____
COMBINE	2 5 3 6 3	_____
DOZEN	8 9 3 5 8 3	_____

LEVEL: ADVANCED

SCATTER PLATTER

YOU HAVE 20 CARDS. ON THE MAIN SIDE THERE IS A **WORD**. ON THE BACK OF EACH CARD ARE ONE SYNONYM AND ONE ANTONYM THAT MATCH THE MAIN WORD.

Cut out or photocopy the cards.

After practising the words, place them with the main word facing up on the table. Look at them altogether for a few minutes.

The first player should then remove three of the cards. The other player(s) then must guess which cards have been removed.

Players can score one point for guessing correctly the missing word, one point for the synonym, and one point for the antonym.

It is not necessary to use all the cards in every game.

constant	passive
wholesome	absurd
restrict	torment
squander	naive
anxious	baffle

accepting active	non-stop temporary
ridiculous sensible	healthy impure
bother comfort	limit loosen
innocent experienced	waste save
confound enlighten	nervous calm

bend	common
agitated	compel
coarse	notice
accept	swollen
weak	private

familiar rare	warp straighten
oblige discourage	perturbed calm
regard ignore	rough smooth
bloated deflated	agree reject
confidential public	frail robust

| LEVEL: EXPERT |

SYNONYM MAZE

This is a maze of synonyms. From the start position <u>words can go forwards, backwards, up or down</u>, but each word is always in a straight line, but not overlapping. Follow the journey from **Start** so that **each new word is a synonym of the previous word**. Note: the next word may use a different meaning from the previous word.

The first two steps have been completed for you. You will finish at END.

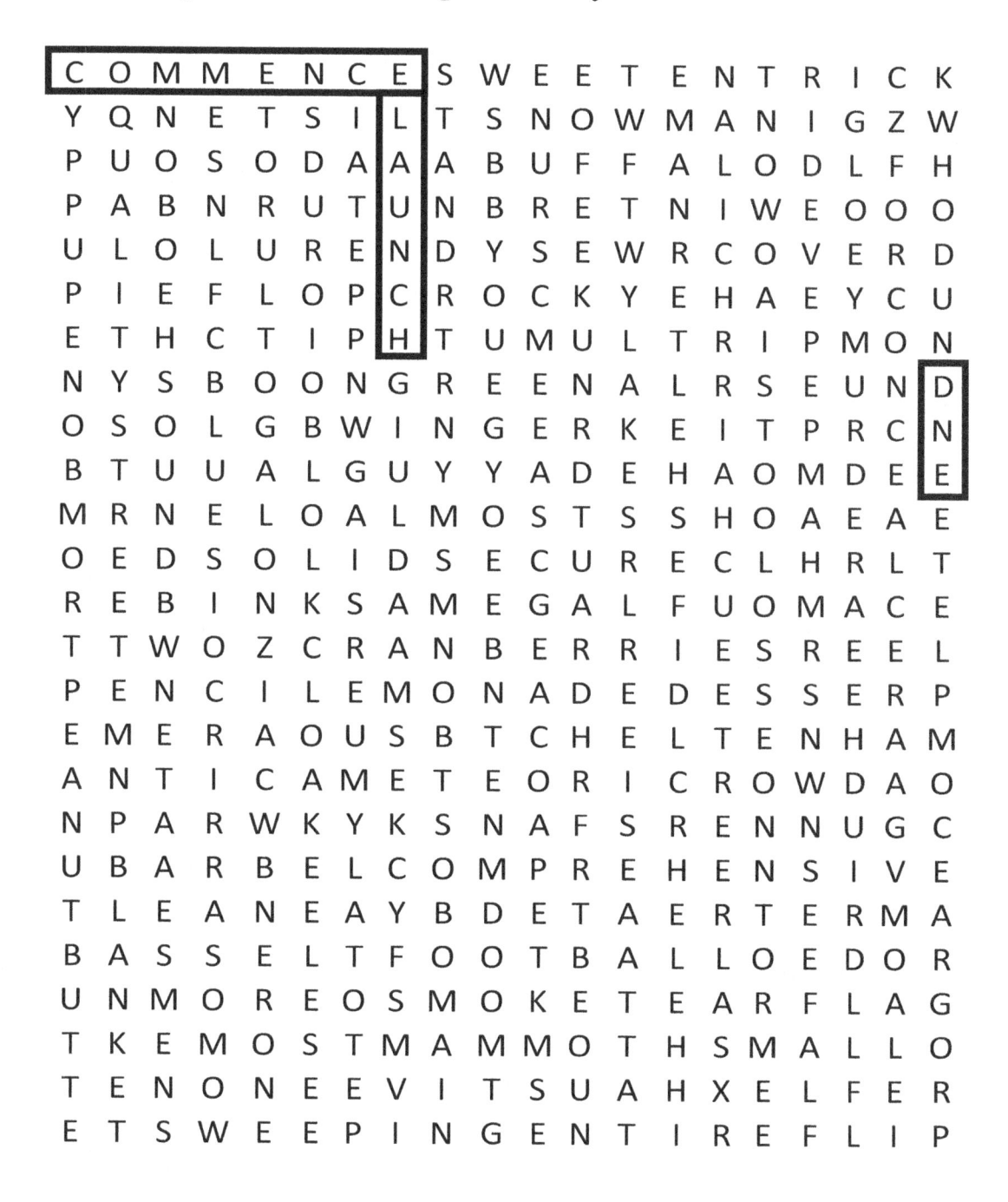

```
C O M M E N C E S W E E T E N T R I C K
Y Q N E T S I L T S N O W M A N I G Z W
P U O S O D A A B U F F A L O D L F H
P A B N R U T U N B R E T N I W E O O O
U L O L U R E N D Y S E W R C O V E R D
P I E F L O P C R O C K Y E H A E Y C U
E T H C T I P H T U M U L T R I P M O N
N Y S B O O N G R E E N A L R S E U N D
O S O L G B W I N G E R K E I T P R C N
B T U U A L G U Y Y A D E H A O M D E E
M R N E L O A L M O S T S S H O A E A E
O E D S O L I D S E C U R E C L H R L T
R E B I N K S A M E G A L F U O M A C E
T T W O Z C R A N B E R R I E S R E E L
P E N C I L E M O N A D E D E S S E R P
E M E R A O U S B T C H E L T E N H A M
A N T I C A M E T E O R I C R O W D A O
N P A R W K Y K S N A F S R E N N U G C
U B A R B E L C O M P R E H E N S I V E
T L E A N E A Y B D E T A E R T E R M A
B A S S E L T F O O T B A L L O E D O R
U N M O R E O S M O K E T E A R F L A G
T K E M O S T M A M M O T H S M A L L O
T E N O N E E V I T S U A H X E L F E R
E T S W E E P I N G E N T I R E F L I P
```

| LEVEL: ADVANCED | # ODD **ONE** OUT |

Find the word that doesn't belong in the following sentences.

Example

HOAX   SHAM   (GENUINE)   FORGERY   COPY

1. CLARIFY   HAZY   HIDDEN   OBSCURE   VAGUE

2. HIGH-TOP   PUMP   BERET   STILETTO   SANDAL

3. POINTLESS   USELESS   WEAK   INEPT   CAPABLE

4. WOOL   NYLON   COTTON   SILK   HEMP

5. STILL   ERRATIC   CALM   STABLE   CONSTANT

6. MOTIVATED   IDLE   PURPOSEFUL   ACTIVE   KEEN

7. MIMIC   REPEAT   ORIGINATE   COPY   RE-DO

8. POSITIVE   AUSPICIOUS   OMINOUS   ENCOURAGING   PROMISING

9. HUB   PERIPHERY   CENTER   INNERMOST   MIDDLE

10. SUPPORT   DISCOURAGE   PROMOTE   BOLSTER   ADVOCATE

ODD **ONE** OUT

11. ELDERLY　　　INFANTILE　　　YOUNG　　　JUNIOR　　　IMMATURE

12. SAW　　　HAMMER　　　CHISEL　　　SCREW DRIVER　　　NAIL

13. LIMB　　　HEART　　　LIVER　　　KIDNEY　　　STOMACH

14. INCISION　　　CLOSE　　　KNIT　　　HEAL　　　STITCH　　　PATCH

15. CROCODILE　　　ALLIGATOR　　　TURTLE　　　LIZARD　　　SALAMANDER

16. DEMOLISH　　DESTROY　　RUIN　　ANNIHILATE　　RENOVATE　　PULVERIZE

17. PERISCOPE　　　MICROSCOPE　　　CAMERA　　　TELEVISION　　　CONTACT

18. HAMMER　　　DISCUS　　　ARROW　　　DISCUSS　　　SHOT PUT

19. CRAVAT　　　CAP　　　BOWLER　　　BONNET　　　FEDORA　　　BEANIE

20. DWELLING　　　SHELTER　　　TEAK　　　TENT　　　TEPEE

21. MAIZE　　　TOMATO　　　POTATO　　　AUBERGINE　　　BAGUETTE

22. SECONDARY　　　SUBSIDIARY　　　JUNIOR　　　CHIEF　　　ASSISTANT

23. OBVIOUS　　　OVERT　　　OBSCURE　　　OPEN　　　APPARENT　　　CLEAR

24. ACCUMULATE　　　GATHER　　　ASSEMBLE　　　CONTRACT　　　ACCRUE

LEVEL: BEGINNER

Synonym Shake

Cut out the cards and shape, which forms a 10-sided die, or decahedron. Fold and stick (or tape) the flaps to make the shape as shown below.

Draw one of the five cards (globe, grab, curve, crowd, question) then toss the decahedron. Use the glossary to check.

If the word facing up on the decahedron has the same meaning as the word on the card, you score a point.

First player to ten points wins.

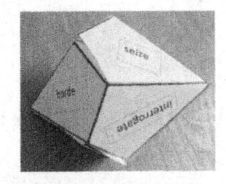

	Player 1	Player 2
Game 1		
Game 2		
Game 3		
Game 4		

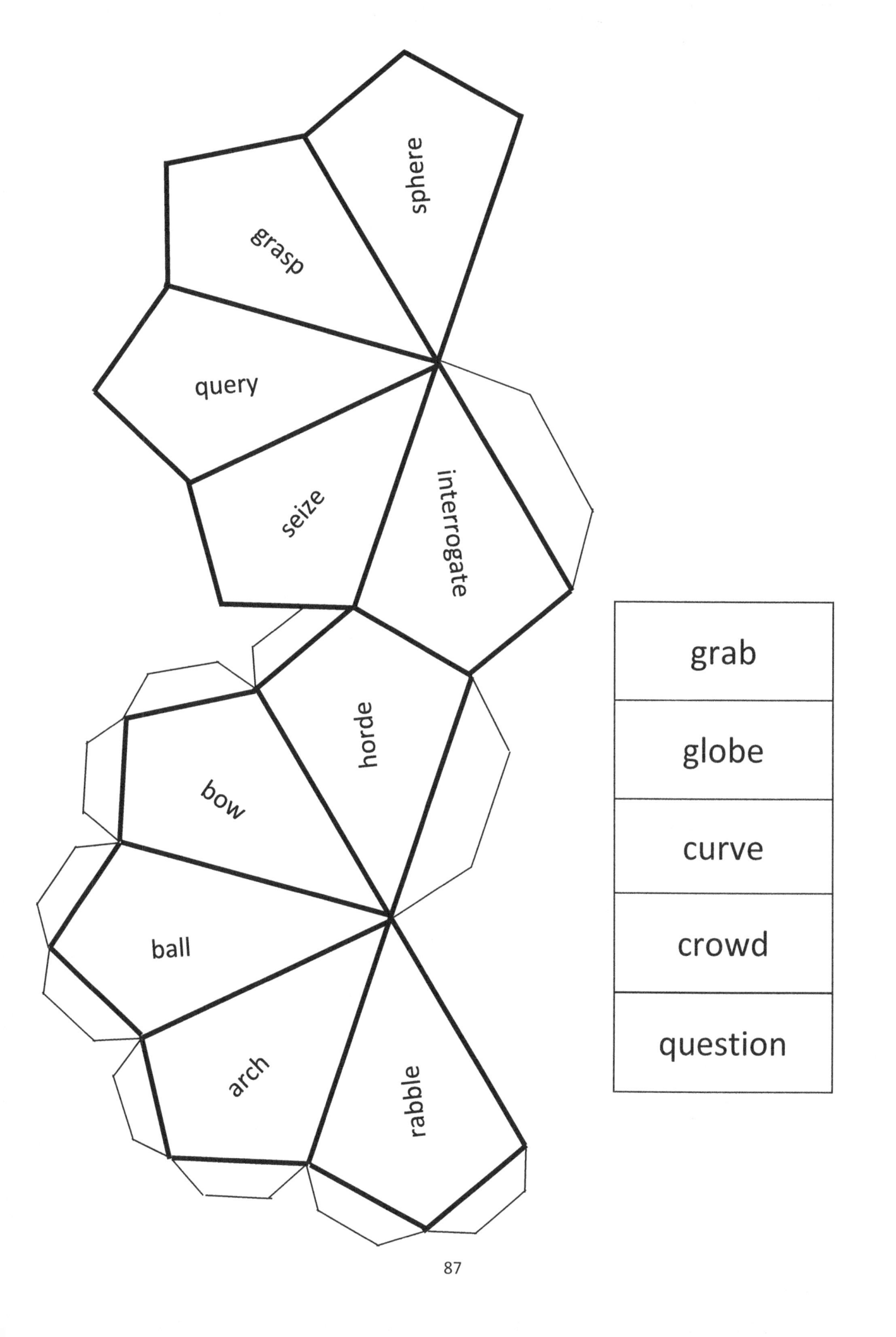

Net labels: sphere, grasp, query, seize, interrogate, horde, bow, ball, arch, rabble

grab
globe
curve
crowd
question

87

This page left intentionally blank!

LEVEL: BEGINNER

Being Instrumental

Where would you most likely find these different instruments? Match the words to the place you would most likely find them.

Hospital **Concert Hall** **Factory**

STETHOSCOPE   SOPRANO

VICE   SCALPEL

PICCOLO   ANVIL

TRIANGLE   SYRINGE

JIGSAW   PIPETTE

CASTANETS   PLIERS

FORCEPS   BASSOON

CHISEL   CYMBALS

VIOLIN   X-RAY

TIMPANI   VENTILATOR

LEVEL: ADVANCED

Hang On Man!

We take a departure from the old game of Hangman to a more hopeful Hang On, Man! Spend some time discovering the meanings of the words on the next page before you play.

The player drawing first starts by choosing a word. On a piece of paper, draw spaces for each of the letters in the word. The other player has to guess a letter. If the guess is correct, then write the letter in the appropriate space(s). If the player misses a letter, draw one part of the Hang On Man. Keep going until the player can guess the word and give its meaning.

If the player misses 7 tries, then the stick figure is complete and they lose that round. You can also use more words from the glossary.

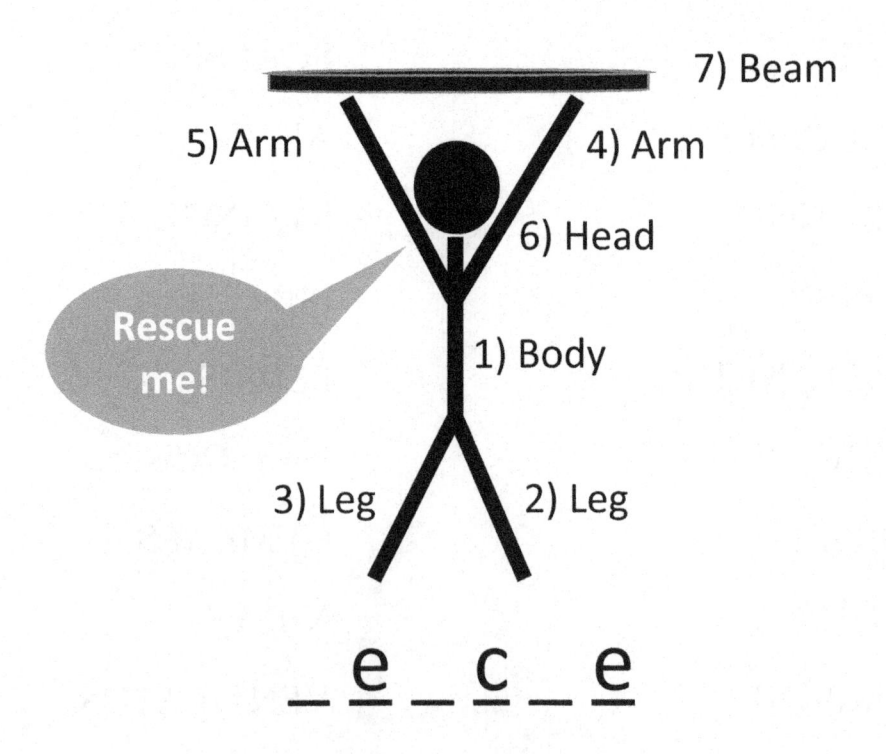

7) Beam
5) Arm
4) Arm
6) Head
Rescue me!
1) Body
3) Leg
2) Leg

_ e _ c _ e

Hang On Man!

LIST A	LIST B
taboo	revolt
exhale	immigrate
deceitful	petroleum
priority	reinforce
thwart	sarcasm
fierce	martyr
flippant	affable
imply	strife
despot	illegible
voluntary	concur
origin	lofty
coarse	glutton
compassion	enigma
guise	gist
spectrum	chaos
extract	surplus
cacophony	shroud
strategy	escalate
perish	pique
adjacent	methodical

Hang On Man!

Hang On Man!

Hang On Man!

LEVEL:
ADVANCED

FIVE POINTS

In this game, use the clues to prompt the player to guess the key word. There are five clues that should lead to the correct answer.

Start with clue 5, if the player guesses on that clue they receive 10 points. If a player guesses on clue 4, they receive 4 points; clue 3 = 3 points; clue 2 = 2 points; clue 1 = 1 point.

EDGE	**PUZZLE**	**DREAM**
1. Fence 2. Ring 3. Boundary 4. Enclosure 5. Perimeter	1. Riddle 2. Confuse 3. Baffle 4. Perplex 5. Conundrum	1. Imagine 2. Fantasy 3. Thought 4. Delusion 5. Trance
HOME	**EXCITING**	**FIND**
1. House 2. Lodging 3. Dwelling 4. Residence 5. Sanctuary	1. Wild 2. Dramatic 3. Thrilling 4. Exhilarating 5. Stimulating	1. Discover 2. Treasure Trove 3. Unearth 4. Detect 5. Acquisition

FIVE POINTS

EXPENSIVE 1. Overpriced 2. Costly 3. Extravagant 4. Excessive 5. Exorbitant	**LUCKY** 1. Favorable 2. Fortunate 3. Charmed 4. Fortuitous 5. Auspicious	**CLEVER** 1. Intelligent 2. Brilliant 3. Gifted 4. Cunning 5. Adroit
SHARP 1. Pointy 2. Prickly 3. Jagged 4. Acute 5. Whetted	**WATER** 1. Rain 2. Liquid 3. Sleet 4. Moisture 5. Precipitation	**HUNGRY** 1. Starving 2. Unsatisfied 3. Craving 4. Famished 5. Ravenous

LEVEL: BEGINNER

Nonsense Poetry

A play on words can make you laugh if you know the right vocabulary. Can you make sense of this poetry?

Can a dual have two fighters – one against another?

Do we enjoy desert when left alone?

Do cops in a forest really exist?

Can a flea get away on its own?

What did the bald baby crying do?

Take a cue and wait for a while,

Can a tree take a bow, or a colonel a nut?

Feet may outperform if they hop for a mile

Can a tropical tree stand in the hand?

A friendly drink would be nice,

Does a harp keep chattering on and on?

Let's not die, let's dice!

LEVEL: BEGINNER

Hidden Link

Find the vertical word linking all of the other words

1).
```
         S C H O L A R
               E D U C A T E
           T E A C H E R
           T U T O R
P E D A G O G U E
         I N S T R U C T O R
         M A S T E R
T R A I N E R
```

2)
```
                     C A N N Y
                   C A R E
                 P R U D E N C E
             A T T E N T I O N
D E L I B E R A T I O N
                 T H O U G H T
             V I G I L A N C E
```

3)
```
         D I S F I G U R E
         I M P A I R
D E S T R O Y
D E M O L I S H
D E F I L E
```

98

Hidden Link

4)
```
    C H A N G E
    M O D I F Y
      T A I L O R
  S H A P E
    A L T E R
```

5)
```
  S P R E A D
  S T R E T C H
    L A T I T U D E
    C A P A C I T Y
    H O R I Z O N
```

6)
```
            A
            I N C O G N I T O
  P S E U D O
            U N I D E N T I F I E D
            M Y S T E R I O U S
  U N N A M E D
            J O H N D O E
            U N C R E D I T E D
            S E C R E T
```

BONUS – Match the word below that goes best with each set:

INTRIGUE   UNIVERSITY   SCAR   DISTANCE
MORPH   CONSIDERATION

LEVEL: BEGINNER

Kooky Cartoons

USE THESE CARTOONS TO HELP YOU REMEMBER THE WORDS. CAN YOU DRAW SOME OF YOUR OWN TOO?

The turning bull was **turbulent**

The great ant allowed his army a holiday **(grant)**

The wind became little **(dwindle)**

Kooky Cartoons

Rob busted out of the jail with all his strength **(robust)**

The place where Cid sat was calm and peaceful **(placid)**

Anna took a cab to the **cabana**

The orange pig meant it was a surprise to everyone **(pigment)**

This ram keeps ambling over the field **(ramble)**

LEVEL: EXPERT
Missing Word Sentences

Fill in the missing word using the words from the list:

Word List

ebb	frequent	caricatures
ceased	casual	guarantee
exterior	adversity	sleek
gullible	chaotic	economize
immense	scrawny	abandon
obvious	embezzled	assembled
fortunate	decay	

1) The accountant had _____ a fortune from the bank before the detectives caught her.

2) The family needed to _____ as times were hard.

3) There is no _____ of safety at the water park, you must be careful.

4) The owner was very proud of his _____ new sports car.

5) The hockey player _____ competing because of his injury.

6) It was _____ that days were getting shorter as it was dark by 5:00 PM.

7) It is _____ in the train station as many passengers are waiting for delayed trains.

102

Missing Word Sentences

8) The campers had to _____ their tent because it had leaked during the storm.

9) Jill is very _____ and believes everything that her friends tell her.

10) Tooth _____ can cause serious health problems.

11) To overcome _____, you must face up to your challenges

12) The _____ and flow of the tide is very relaxing.

13) The _____ of the house was more beautiful than the interior.

14) Dean is a _____ visitor to the cinema as he loves films.

15) Freda is good at drawing cartoons and her _____ are very funny.

16) The king was thin and _____, but the people loved him.

17) Noah was _____ to be picked for the team.

18) The school _____ in the gym.

19) It was with _____ pride that the team held up the winners' trophy.

20) The man is wearing _____ clothes: jeans, a T-Shirt, and sneakers.

LEVEL: BEGINNER

Ridiculous Rhymes

Read the ridiculous rhymes below. Let these rhymes help you remember the definitions of the key words given.

Key Words
accumulate, arrogant, morose, conceal, admire, distinct, volatile, esteem, hesitate, embark, allocate, fatal, flaw, incognito, lexicon, constrict, hapless, poise, prohibit, emphasize, signify

1. Grandma loved to accumulate
   Over one thousand cups and plates!

2. Tina was such an arrog-ant
   She boasted to the eleph-ant

3. The morose gent could not conceal
   The romantic heartache he did feel

4. The horses they did all admire
   The unicorn singing in the choir

5. Rasheed's look was quite distinct
   Perhaps it was the way he winked

6. The volcano's mood was so volatile
   The villagers ran for half a mile

7. The player was held in great esteem
   When he scored a touchdown for the team

8. Harry hamster wasn't one to hesitate
   Her greatest fear was being too late

Ridiculous Rhymes

9. On a perilous journey did Sam embark
   But lost his footing in the dark

10. Ted was having difficulty trying to allocate
    Sufficient time to write a report on Alexander The Great

11. Mildred's plan had a fatal flaw
    Space travel with zebras was against international law

12. Amongst the thousands of people, did no one know
    The movie star in the hat and sunglasses was incognito

13. Hours of vocabulary practice she had done
    She began to feel like a lexicon

14. The snake liked to tighten and constrict
    The hapless victim she had picked

15. The ballerina had such perfect poise
    She pirouetted above the noise

16. I'm certain that we must prohibit
    Lions singing at the exhibit

17. At work Simon liked to emphasize
    His unique style by wearing colorful ties

18. The leaking faucet did signify
    A future shortage in the water supply

LEVEL: BEGINNER

STORY BUILDER

A fun game for two players. Each player has a list of 20 words.

In this exercise, you will create a story based on a sentence from the previous player.

You must use at least one of the words in your list in each sentence.

Use only one connective word (AND, OR, ALSO, BUT) per sentence.

The winner is the first player to use all of their words, although this activity is really about working together.

Once

upon

a

time...

LIST 1

shabby	modern
delayed	sketch
fret	labyrinth
nimble	agile
hinder	charge
scent	blank
trivial	alter
minor	major
ferocious	vex
abundance	oasis

STORY BUILDER	STORY BUILDER
STORY BUILDER	STORY BUILDER
STORY BUILDER	STORY BUILDER
STORY BUILDER	STORY BUILDER
STORY BUILDER	STORY BUILDER
STORY BUILDER	STORY BUILDER
STORY BUILDER	STORY BUILDER
STORY BUILDER	STORY BUILDER
STORY BUILDER	STORY BUILDER
STORY BUILDER	STORY BUILDER

LIST 2

primary	intercept
fiction	saunter
kin	tolerate
unruly	internal
grave	plethora
ancestor	adapt
solemn	foe
peak	inquire
defy	pliable
contradict	unravel

STORY BUILDER	STORY BUILDER
STORY BUILDER	STORY BUILDER
STORY BUILDER	STORY BUILDER
STORY BUILDER	STORY BUILDER
STORY BUILDER	STORY BUILDER
STORY BUILDER	STORY BUILDER
STORY BUILDER	STORY BUILDER
STORY BUILDER	STORY BUILDER
STORY BUILDER	STORY BUILDER
STORY BUILDER	STORY BUILDER

LEVEL: BEGINNER

Professionally Speaking

Can you identify what these people do? Match the profession on the left with what they do on the right column.

PHYSICIAN	Makes maps
PHARMACIST	Studies the economy
ENGINEER	Makes arrangements at a funeral
ARCHAEOLOGIST	Sells houses and property
ARCHITECT	Handles and carries luggage
CARTOGRAPHER	Doctor
COSMETOLOGIST	Greets clients at an office
DIETICIAN	Digs up and studies artifacts
ECONOMIST	Fixes leaks
MORTICIAN	Designs machines or structures
GLAZIER	Designs buildings
PORTER	Helps to straighten teeth
RECEPTIONIST	Provides emergency medical care
FARRIER	Practices law in a court
STENOGRAPHER	Makes and repairs clothing
ORTHODONTIST	Dispenses medicine
PARAMEDIC	Fits glass into windows and doors
PLUMBER	Makes and repairs things in iron
ATTORNEY	A person who gives beauty treatments
TAILOR	Makes and repairs wooden objects
REAL ESTATE AGENT	Expert on diet and nutrition
BLACKSMITH	A person who transcribes speech in shorthand
CARPENTER	Makes shoes for horses

LEVEL: EXPERT

WHALE OF A TALE

Find where the missing words go in the following excerpt from Herman Melville's classic story *Moby Dick*.

morbid	calamities	circulate	hereditary	exaggerate
latitudes	panic	remotest	adequate	rumors
perils	fortitude			

And as for those who, previously hearing of the White Whale, by chance caught sight of him; in the beginning of the thing they had every one of them, almost, as boldly and fearlessly lowered for him, as for any other whale of that species. But at length, such ____1____ did ensue in these assaults—not restricted to sprained wrists and ankles, broken limbs, or devouring amputations—but fatal to the last degree of fatality; those repeated disastrous repulses, all accumulating and piling their terrors upon Moby Dick; those things had gone far to shake the ____2____ of many brave hunters, to whom the story of the White Whale had eventually come.

Nor did wild rumors of all sorts fail to ____3____, and still the more horrify the true histories of these deadly encounters. For not only do fabulous rumors naturally grow out of the very body of all surprising terrible events,—as the smitten tree gives birth to its fungi; but, in maritime life, far more than in that of terra firma, wild ____4____ abound, wherever there is any ____5____ reality for them to cling to. And as the sea surpasses the land in this matter, so the whale fishery surpasses every other sort of maritime life, in the wonderfulness and fearfulness of the rumors which sometimes ____6____ there.

WHALE OF A TALE

For not only are whalemen as a body unexempt from that ignorance and superstitiousness ___7___ to all sailors; but of all sailors, they are by all odds the most directly brought into contact with whatever is appallingly astonishing in the sea; face to face they not only eye its greatest marvels, but, hand to jaw, give battle to them.

Alone, in such ___8___ waters, that though you sailed a thousand miles, and passed a thousand shores, you would not come to any chiseled hearthstone, or aught hospitable beneath that part of the sun; in such ___9___ and longitudes, pursuing too such a calling as he does, the whaleman is wrapped by influences all tending to make his fancy pregnant with many a mighty birth.

No wonder, then, that ever gathering volume from the mere transit over the widest watery spaces, the outblown rumors of the White Whale did in the end incorporate with themselves all manner of ___10___ hints, and half-formed suggestions of supernatural agencies, which eventually invested Moby Dick with new terrors unborrowed from anything that visibly appears. So that in many cases such a ___11___ did he finally strike, that few who by those rumors, at least, had heard of the White Whale, few of those hunters were willing to encounter the ___12___ of his jaw.

LEVEL: ADVANCED

WORD SEARCH III
SENSES

Can you match these words with the matching related sense?
(SMELL / HEAR / TASTE / FEEL / SEE)

	SMELL	HEAR	TASTE	FEEL	SEE
1. AROMA					
2. CONTACT					
3. PIQUANT					
4. CACOPHONY					
5. GRAZE					
6. WITNESS					
7. FRAGRANT					
8. EAVESDROP					
9. CARESS					
10. STENCH					
11. PALATE					
12. VIBRATION					
13. DETECT					
14. BOUQUET					
15. HARK					
16. TANG					

WORD SEARCH – SENSES

Find these words in the word search below:

AROMA	CONTACT	FRAGRANT	DETECT
PIQUANT	CACOPHONY	EAVESDROP	BOUQUET
GRAZE	WITNESS	VIBRATION	HARK
CARESS	STENCH	PALATE	TANG

```
A  R  O  M  C  A  C  O  P  H  O  N  Y  B
K  L  B  T  R  D  E  T  A  C  T  F  G  O
C  A  C  O  P  S  T  E  N  C  H  R  H  U
S  D  M  T  U  D  R  O  P  I  A  A  L  Q
S  A  R  O  M  Q  U  I  C  Z  J  G  O  E
E  Z  A  R  Q  T  U  L  E  W  O  R  P  Y
N  Y  E  W  I  T  N  E  R  A  L  A  S  T
T  C  A  T  N  O  C  D  T  E  F  N  S  I
I  L  V  D  K  P  L  E  T  C  E  T  E  D
W  B  E  P  Q  R  U  N  G  F  G  M  R  N
P  A  S  A  T  E  A  V  E  T  A  L  A  P
H  A  D  K  Q  U  A  H  O  G  L  A  C  E
T  N  R  F  Q  U  E  T  E  N  D  E  H  B
A  P  O  I  P  N  O  I  T  A  R  B  I  V
A  C  P  H  O  N  Y  W  I  T  N  E  S  T
```

LEVEL: BEGINNER

Snap!

Cut out the cards on the following pages. All cards should be shuffled and placed in a central pile face down. The players take turns lifting up a card, placing it face up so that all can see, creating a row of cards.

If a card is lifted from the main stack of cards, that is the same word as one of any of the cards already lifted, the first player to say "Snap!" and to give two different meanings of the word, gets to keep that pair of cards.

Examples:

WIND – a gust of air
WIND – to turn

BALL – a round object used in games
BALL – a formal event with dancing

The winner is the player with the most pairs of cards after all cards have been lifted.

ball	ball
bear	bear
boot	boot
case	case
counter	counter
dash	dash
duck	duck
firm	firm
jam	jam
lap	lap

Snap!	Snap!
Snap!	Snap!
Snap!	Snap!
Snap!	Snap!
Snap!	Snap!
Snap!	Snap!
Snap!	Snap!
Snap!	Snap!
Snap!	Snap!
Snap!	Snap!

bat	bat
charge	charge
bow	bow
console	console
cover	cover
foil	foil
fair	fair
grant	grant
key	key
nail	nail

Snap!	Snap!
Snap!	Snap!
Snap!	Snap!
Snap!	Snap!
Snap!	Snap!
Snap!	Snap!
Snap!	Snap!
Snap!	Snap!
Snap!	Snap!
Snap!	Snap!

match	match
object	object
palm	palm
pride	pride
pack	pack
raw	raw
rigid	rigid
sound	sound
subject	subject
tear	tear

Snap!	Snap!
Snap!	Snap!
Snap!	Snap!
Snap!	Snap!
Snap!	Snap!
Snap!	Snap!
Snap!	Snap!
Snap!	Snap!
Snap!	Snap!
Snap!	Snap!

LEVEL: EXPERT

Anagrams

Look at the anagram on the left. Rearrange the letters so that you create a new word or phrase. The first has been done as an example.

	Clue	*Answer*
NEED O CAT	Short, interesting story	ANECDOTE
VIE A CAR	Extreme greed	_____
VOTER	Open, not concealed	_____
TEN NILE	Tolerant, lax	_____
PAY HAT	Disinterest	_____
TROUT	Teacher	_____
RENT STING	Strict	_____
YES RAT END	Inactive	_____
CEE CAB LIMP	Flawless	_____
ICE TIN	Stir up trouble	_____
SOUL CAL	Insensitive	_____
MEAT PEER	To spread throughout	_____
NOD CAR	Honesty	_____
IF OR CLIP	Productive	_____
RAG IS OUR EGG	Outgoing	_____

LEVEL: ADVANCED

SQUARE ROOTS

This is a game that will assist you in learning common root words. It will help you to work out many more unfamiliar terms. Before you begin, spend some time looking at the root words and their meanings on page 116.

How to play: Cut out the cards, shuffle them and place them in a pile. Use the dot grid.

Players take turns drawing cards. If they can correctly provide the meaning of the root word on the card, then they can draw a line joining two dots on the grid.

As in the traditional game of squares, players attempt to complete a square and write their initial inside.

There are 20 root words on the cards. Once all of the cards have been used, shuffle them and start again until the grid has been completely filled with squares.

The winner will have completed the most squares.

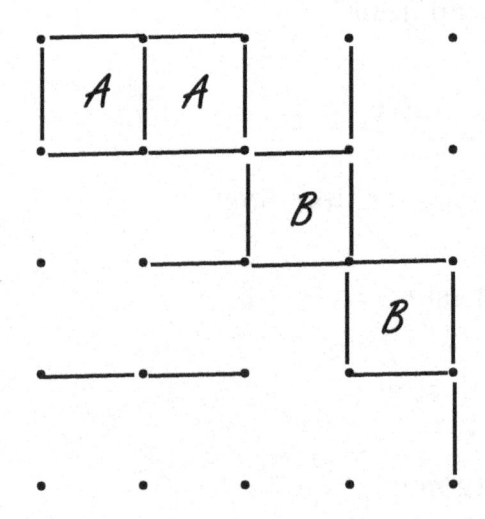

AUDIO	CHROMO
POLY	PHOTO
SPHERE	BIO
GEO	LOGO
PHONE	SCOPE
MAL	BEN
BI	HYPER
HYPO	ANTI
ANTE	SUB
SYN	UNI

SQUARE ROOTS	SQUARE ROOTS
SQUARE ROOTS	SQUARE ROOTS
SQUARE ROOTS	SQUARE ROOTS
SQUARE ROOTS	SQUARE ROOTS
SQUARE ROOTS	SQUARE ROOTS
SQUARE ROOTS	SQUARE ROOTS
SQUARE ROOTS	SQUARE ROOTS
SQUARE ROOTS	SQUARE ROOTS
SQUARE ROOTS	SQUARE ROOTS
SQUARE ROOTS	SQUARE ROOTS

SQUARE ROOTS

ROOT WORD MEANINGS

MAL – bad

HYPER – over

BIO – life

PHOTO – light

BI – two

CHROMO – color

UNI – one

GEO – earth

POLY – many

ANTI – against

BEN – good

SYN – same

PHONE – sound

SPHERE – ball

ANTE – before

HYPO – under

LOGO – word/reason

AUDIO – hear

SCOPE – see

SUB – under

SQUARE ROOTS

GAME GRID

SQUARE ROOTS

GAME GRID

LEVEL: EXPERT

OUT OF TIME

Read the following passage from H.G. Wells famous novel *The Time Machine*. Some of the words have been taken and re-used in the sentences afterward. Can you find the right words?

****

The thing the Time Traveller held in his hand was a glittering metallic **framework**, scarcely larger than a small clock, and very delicately made.

There was ivory in it, and some **transparent** crystalline substance. And now I must be **explicit**, for this that follows—unless his explanation is to be accepted—is an absolutely unaccountable thing. He took one of the small octagonal tables that were scattered about the room, and set it in front of the fire, with two legs on the hearthrug.

On this table he placed the **mechanism**. Then he drew up a chair, and sat down. The only other object on the table was a small shaded lamp, the bright light of which fell upon the model.

There were also perhaps a dozen candles about, two in brass candlesticks upon the **mantel** and several in sconces, so that the room was brilliantly **illuminated**. I sat in a low arm-chair nearest the fire, and I drew this forward so as to be almost between the Time Traveller and the fireplace. Filby sat behind him, looking over his shoulder. The Medical Man and the Provincial Mayor watched him in **profile** from the right, the Psychologist from the left.

The Very Young Man stood behind the Psychologist. We were all on the alert. It appears incredible to me that any kind of trick, however **subtly** conceived and however **adroitly** done, could have been played upon us under these conditions.

The Time Traveller looked at us, and then at the mechanism. "Well?" said the Psychologist.

OUT OF TIME

"This little affair," said the Time Traveller, resting his elbows upon the table and pressing his hands together above the **apparatus**, "is only a model. It is my plan for a machine to travel through time. You will notice that it looks singularly **askew**, and that there is an odd twinkling appearance about this bar, as though it was in some way unreal." He pointed to the part with his finger. "Also, here is one little white lever, and here is another."

The Medical Man got up out of his chair and peered into the thing. "It's beautifully made," he said.

"It took two years to make," retorted the Time Traveller. Then, when we had all imitated the action of the Medical Man, he said: "Now I want you clearly to understand that this lever, being pressed over, sends the machine gliding into the future, and this other reverses the motion. This saddle represents the seat of a time traveller. Presently I am going to press the lever, and off the machine will go. It will **vanish**, pass into future Time, and disappear. Have a good look at the thing. Look at the table too, and satisfy yourselves there is no trickery. I don't want to waste this model, and then be told I'm a quack."

There was a minute's pause perhaps. The Psychologist seemed about to speak to me, but changed his mind. Then the Time Traveller put forth his finger towards the lever. "No," he said suddenly. "Lend me your hand." And turning to the Psychologist, he took that individual's hand in his own and told him to put out his forefinger. So that it was the Psychologist himself who sent forth the model Time Machine on its **interminable** voyage. We all saw the lever turn. I am absolutely certain there was no trickery. There was a breath of wind, and the lamp flame jumped.

One of the candles on the mantel was blown out, and the little machine suddenly swung round, became **indistinct**, was seen as a ghost for a second perhaps, as an eddy of faintly glittering brass and ivory; and it was gone—vanished! Save for the lamp the table was bare.

OUT OF TIME

1. The packaging _____ on the assembly line malfunctioned, causing a delay in production.
2. Due to the fading light, Thomas could only see the _____ of the intruder.
3. Deepak _____ navigated the ship through the rough sea.
4. The doctors used a breathing _____ to keep the patient alive.
5. The _____ presentation seemed to go on forever.
6. Molly avoided an argument by _____ changing the subject from politics to the weather.
7. The Constitution provides a general _____ for our system of government.
8. He wore plain, _____ clothing to blend in with the crowd.
9. Tony proudly displayed his award on the fireplace _____.
10. The curtains were _____ and therefore let in the sunlight.
11. The rules were _____, no food was allowed outside of the cafeteria.
12. The jar was _____ by a collection of over fifty fireflies.
13. Not known for his tidy appearance, John usually went to work in a wrinkled shirt and a tie that was _____.
14. Afraid that the cupcakes would _____ before the next day, Linda hid them in the cabinet.

WORD BANK

FRAMEWORK	ADROITLY	APPARATUS	VANISH
MECHANISM	TRANSPARENT	INDISTINCT	ASKEW
MANTEL	INTERMINABLE	ILLUMINATED	EXPLICIT
PROFILE	SUBTLY		

LEVEL: ADVANCED

Idioms

Idioms are expressions that have a different meaning than the literal meaning of the words in the phrase. For example, "What's up?" is a common greeting that is not asking what is in the air, but rather what is going on, what are you doing, or what do you want.

Draw a line from each expression to the best matching meaning below:

Once in a blue moon	Reform
Let the cat out of the bag	Remain silent
Go cold turkey	Slumber
Smell a rat	To not feel well
Mind your Ps & Qs	Something very easy
Hold your tongue	(wishing you) Good Luck
Sling mud	To deceive someone
A feather in your cap	Torrential
Have your heart in your mouth	Face the consequences
Catch 40 winks	To concede, give up
Take the bull by the horns	Delay making a decision
Pull the wool over someone's eyes	Stop or quit a habit suddenly
Turn over a new leaf	To set boundaries
Sit on the fence	To deceive playfully, tease
Pull someone's leg	Be on your best behavior
Break a leg	To be worried or frightened
Blow your own horn	To slander or insult someone
Raining cats and dogs	Reveal a secret
Face the music	To directly confront a difficult situation
Throw in the towel	An achievement
Draw the line	Have a suspicion something is wrong
A piece of cake	Be boastful
Be under the weather	Something that occurs very rarely

LEVEL: ADVANCED

Best Fit

In this exercise, look at the main word in bold. Try to find the word underneath it that best matches the definition.

1. CONFOUND
a. create
b. mystify
c. combine
d. deny

2. DIVERSITY
a. college
b. divided
c. variety
d. devolve

3. EXPOSITION
a. exposure
b. exhibition
c. placement
d. attitude

4. ADJACENT
a. administrative
b. unattached
c. parallel
d. adjoining

5. ELABORATE
a. elevated
b. unsophisticated
c. complex
d. elongated

6. ACCUMULATE
a. diminish
b. gather
c. demand
d. accuse

7. HEROIC
a. gallant
b. terrific
c. marksman
d. decorated

8. ACQUIRE
a. settle
b. give
c. gain
d. grow

9. TENSION
a. calamity
b. savings
c. temple
d. strain

10. PROMINENT
a. conspicuous
b. excited
c. camouflaged
d. perturbed

Best Fit

11. SUBSTITUTE
a. underachieve
b. introduce
c. replacement
d. teacher

12. ANTICIPATE
a. precipitate
b. predict
c. exhaust
d. against

13. RELINQUISH
a. require
b. restore
c. extinguish
d. abdicate

14. EFFORTLESS
a. arduous
b. complexity
c. easy
d. rough

15. CONFLICT
a. harmonious
b. contradict
c. demonstrate
d. construct

16. PRIMARY
a. principle
b. pupil
c. abyss
d. principal

17. APPROXIMATE
a. eradicated
b. esteemed
c. estimated
d. evaporated

18. UNEXPECTED
a. anticipated
b. unforeseen
c. uninvited
d. undivided

19. EQUIVALENT
a. equal
b. unequitable
c. superior
d. divergent

20. ABRUPTLY
a. measured
b. soundly
c. nonchalantly
d. suddenly

LEVEL: BEGINNER

DOT · TO · DOT

Do this dot to dot using the clues given for in order. Use the letters in the answer to connect the dots and complete the picture. The first answer has been given. Use the word bank if you get stuck.

Clues:	**Answer**
not transparent	opaque
desire	_____
neutral	_____
complain	_____
worried	_____
exaggerate	_____
careful with money	_____
outside edge	_____
untidy	_____
magical	_____
throb or move rhythmically	_____
to go into	_____
difficult to carry	_____
changeable personality	_____
stick out	_____
rude	_____
beginner	_____
not urban	_____
go faster	_____

Word Bank: accelerate, bulky, craving, disheveled, economical, embellish, enchanting, fickle, gripe, impertinent, indifferent, novice, opaque, penetrate, perimeter, perturbed, pulsate, protrude, rural

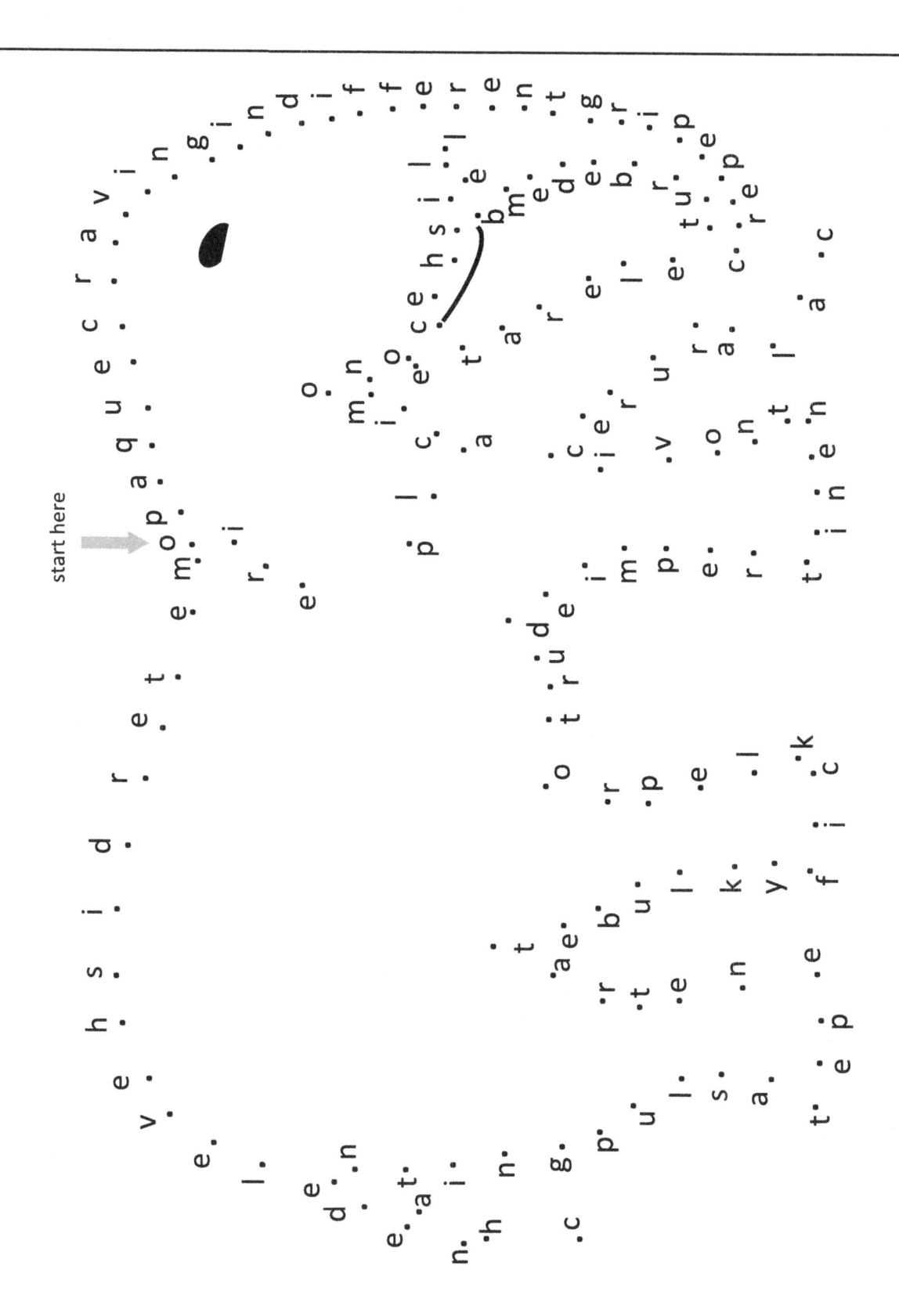

**BONUS QUESTION:
WHAT KIND OF CREATURE AM I?**

ANSWER: _ _ C _ Y _ ER _

137

LEVEL: EXPERT

Missing Letter Antonyms

Fill in the missing letters to find the **antonym**. The first exercise has been done as an example.

1. DRASTIC   C A L M
2. ASSISTANCE   H _ N D _ _ _ N _ _ _
3. TURBULENT   _ E _ T _ E
4. OBEDIENT   I _ S _ L _ _ _ T
5. SHREWD   _ O _ L I _ H
6. OPRESS   A _ _ I _ T
7. ORIGIN   _ O _ C _ U _ I _ _
8. REALISTIC   _ M _ R _ _ _ _ I _ A _
9. INFERIOR   P _ R _ M _ U _ _ _
10. ERADICATE   _ O _ S _ R _ _ _ T
11. MINUSCULE   _ I _ A _ T _ C
12. EXPANSION   C _ _ T _ _ _ T _ O _
13. TEMPORARY   _ _ R _ _ N _ N _
14. FORTIFY   W _ _ _ _ E _
15. PERIMETER   _ E _ T _ _ _
16. CONCEAL   R _ _ E _ _ _
17. HAPLESS   _ O _ _ U _ A _ E
18. FANTASY   R _ A _ I _ _

138

LEVEL: EXPERT

ANTONYM MAZE

This is a maze of antonyms. From the start position words can go forwards, backwards, up or down, but each word is always in a straight line, but not overlapping. Follow the journey from *Start* so that **each new word is a antonym of the previous word**. Note: the next word may use a different meaning from the previous word.

The first two steps have been completed for you. You will finish at END.

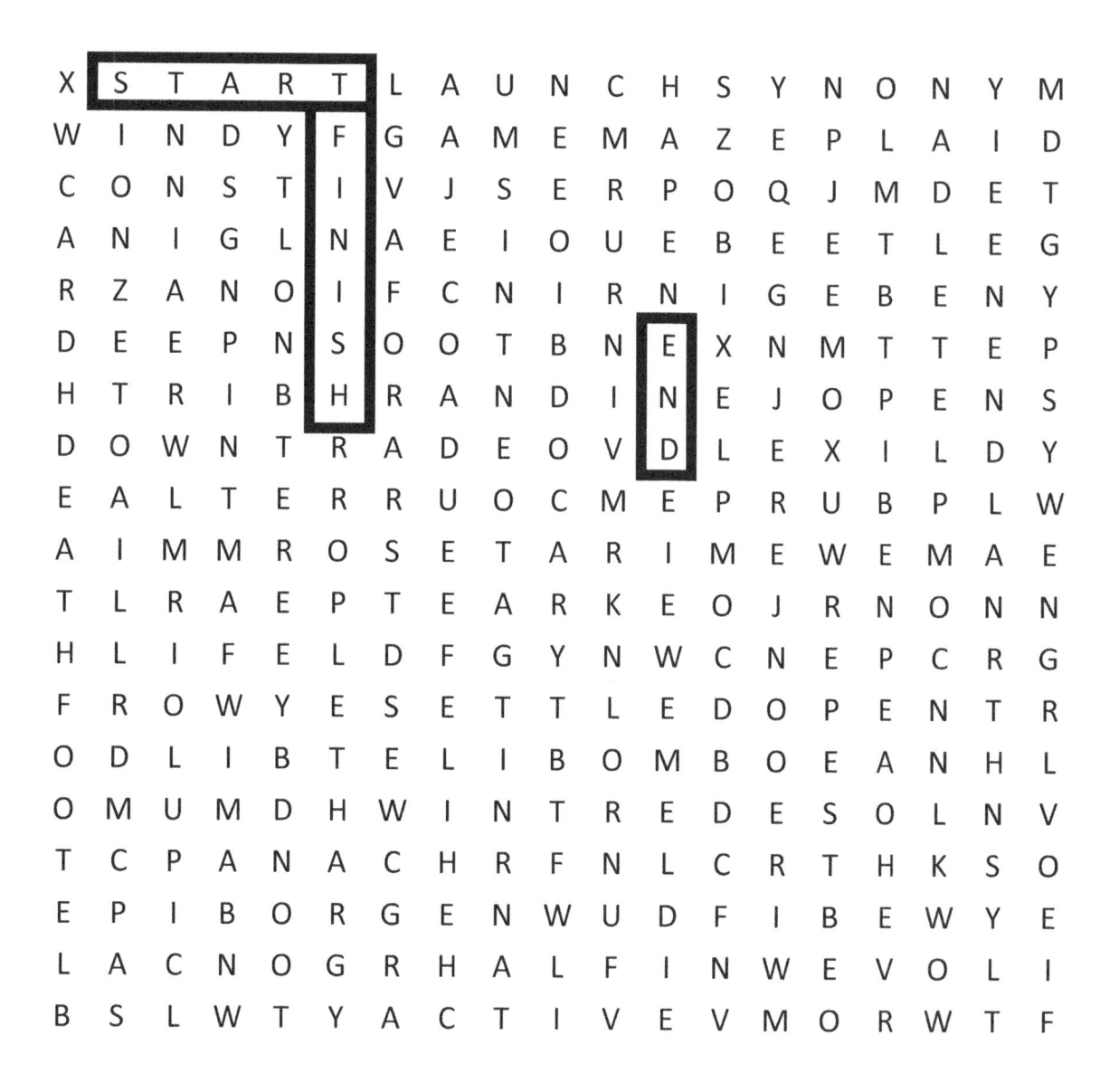

```
X  S  T  A  R  T  L  A  U  N  C  H  S  Y  N  O  N  Y  M
W  I  N  D  Y  F  G  A  M  E  M  A  Z  E  P  L  A  I  D
C  O  N  S  T  I  V  J  S  E  R  P  O  Q  J  M  D  E  T
A  N  I  G  L  N  A  E  I  O  U  E  B  E  E  T  L  E  G
R  Z  A  N  O  I  F  C  N  I  R  N  I  G  E  B  E  N  Y
D  E  E  P  N  S  O  O  T  B  N  E  X  N  M  T  T  E  P
H  T  R  I  B  H  R  A  N  D  I  N  E  J  O  P  E  N  S
D  O  W  N  T  R  A  D  E  O  V  D  L  E  X  I  L  D  Y
E  A  L  T  E  R  R  U  O  C  M  E  P  R  U  B  P  L  W
A  I  M  M  R  O  S  E  T  A  R  I  M  E  W  E  M  A  E
T  L  R  A  E  P  T  E  A  R  K  E  O  J  R  N  O  N  N
H  L  I  F  E  L  D  F  G  Y  N  W  C  N  E  P  C  R  G
F  R  O  W  Y  E  S  E  T  T  L  E  D  O  P  E  N  T  R
O  D  L  I  B  T  E  L  I  B  O  M  B  O  E  A  N  H  L
O  M  U  M  D  H  W  I  N  T  R  E  D  E  S  O  L  N  V
T  C  P  A  N  A  C  H  R  F  N  L  C  R  T  H  K  S  O
E  P  I  B  O  R  G  E  N  W  U  D  F  I  B  E  W  Y  E
L  A  C  N  O  G  R  H  A  L  F  I  N  W  E  V  O  L  I
B  S  L  W  T  Y  A  C  T  I  V  E  V  M  O  R  W  T  F
```

| LEVEL: EXPERT |

Tic Tac Toe

This game is designed to be used to test knowledge of any of the vocabulary used in this book. It can either be played as the traditional 9-box game, or as extreme tic tac toe.

In the regular version, players take turns marking either an X or O in a single grid of nine squares. Before taking a turn, players are challenged to give a definition for any word in the glossary – only the opponent picks the word! If the player guessing can give the correct answer, then they can make a mark. If a player does not know the correct answer, they do not get to make a mark and the next player goes. Players will try to win by getting three Xs or Os in a row, horizontally, vertically or diagonally. The winner of the first five out of nine games will be champion.

The second version (extreme) demands a great deal of strategic thinking. This version uses the whole sheet of nine games, not just a single grid at a time. As in the regular version, players take turns by giving a correct definition or synonym to a glossary word, chosen by their opponent. Players can mark their X or O in any square on the sheet. In effect, you are playing nine games at once! The player who can win three individual grids horizontally, vertically, or diagonally wins the game (See example below).

The game sheets are on the next three pages.

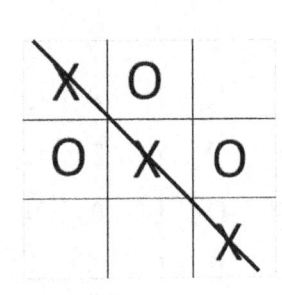

X player winning Regular version

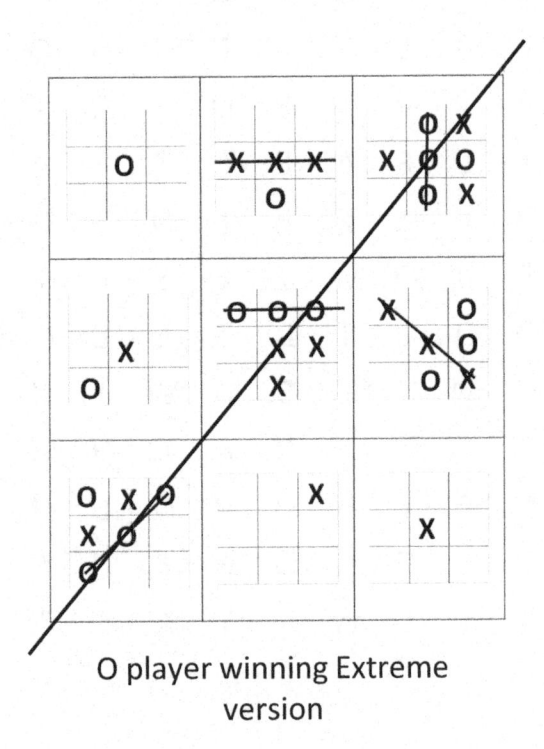

O player winning Extreme version

Tic Tac Toe

Tic Tac Toe

Tic Tac Toe

Glossary

Word	Definition	Seen on Pages
abandon	(verb) to stop supporting and looking after someone; to give up completely; (noun) complete lack of restraint	102
abdicate	(verb) when a king or queen gives up their power; to fail to undertake or avoid responsibility	135
abhorrent	(adjective) morally very bad; dreadful	55
abolish	(verb) to put an end to something officially	49, 70
abrupt	(adjective) sudden and not expected; not friendly or polite	63, 135
absent	(adjective) not present	49
abstain	(verb) to not do something you could do	49
absurd	(adjective) ridiculous; completely unreasonable	79
abundance	(noun) plenty of something; more than is needed	55, 107
accelerate	(verb) to increase speed, go faster	136
accrue	(verb) to increase over a period of time	85
accumulate	(verb) to gather together or collect an increasing amount of something	85, 104, 134
accurate	(adjective) correct; exact	56, 70
achievement	(noun) the act of succeeding in a goal; accomplishment	63, 133
acquire	(verb) to find, get, or receive	19, 70, 134
acquisition	(noun) something bought or obtained; the learning or development of a skill or habit	95
acute	(adjective) very serious, severe; an angle of less than 90 degrees	96
adequate	(adjective) enough or satisfactory for a particular purpose	112
adjacent	(adjective) next to or adjoining something else	14, 91, 134
admire	(verb) to regard with respect	104
adapt	(verb) to change to meet different situations	99, 109
adopt	(verb) to accept or to begin to use something; to legally take a child into your family	9, 38
adroit	(adjective) quick and skillful	96, 130
adversity	(noun) a difficult or unlucky situation or event	38, 102
affable	(adjective) friendly, good natured	34, 91
affiliation	(noun) a connection with a political party or religion, or with a larger organization	55
affluent	(adjective) very wealthy	32, 35
agenda	(noun) a list of matters to be discussed or dealt with; a program of action	38
agile	(adjective) able to move quickly and easily	32, 57, 77, 107
agitated	(adjective) feeling troubled or nervous; annoyed	32, 81
aid	(noun) help or support received; (verb) to help or support	56
aim	(noun) a result your plans are intended to achieve; the act of pointing a weapon toward something; (verb) to point a weapon or other object toward someone or something	38
ajar	(adjective) slightly open	77
alert	(adjective) quick to see, understand, and act; (noun) a warning	24, 70
allocate	(verb) to give something as a share of a total amount; to give a particular amount of time or money, for a specific purpose	105
alter	(verb) to change	9, 36, 99, 107
amass	(verb) to gather a large amount of something	56
ambush	(noun) a sudden surprise attack from a hidden place; (verb) to suddenly attack someone after hiding and waiting for them	59
amiable	(adjective) friendly and easy going	34, 61
amicable	(adjective) friendly	49

Word	Definition	Seen on Pages
amphibian	(noun) a type of animal that lives both on land and in water	26, 56
amulet	(noun) a lucky charm or object worn to protect against evil or bad luck	51
analyze	(verb) to study something in a systematic and careful way	14
ancestor	(noun) a person related to you who lived a long time ago	109
anchor	(noun) a heavy metal object that keeps a boat from moving; someone who gives support when needed; a person who reports the news; (verb) to lower an anchor in the water to keep a boat from moving; to make something stay in one position by fastening it firmly	61
anecdote	(noun) a short, often amusing story	123
anonymous	(adjective) without a name that is known or made public	99
antagonize	(verb) to anger someone greatly	35
ante-	(root) before	125, 127
anthology	(noun) a collection of selected writings	22
anti-	(root) against	125, 127
anticipate	(verb) to regard a probable; expect, predict	135
anvil	(noun) a heavy block of iron on which heated pieces of metal are made into a particular shape with a hammer	89
anxious	(adjective) worried and nervous; wanting very much for something to happen	12. 79
apathy	(noun) a lack of interest; unwilling to take action	123
appalled	(adjective) having strong feelings of shock and disgust	56
apparatus	(noun) a set of equipment, tools, or a machine that is used for a particular purpose	131, 132
apparent	(adjective) able to be seen or understood; seeming to be true	85
apple	(noun) a round, edible fruit having a red, green, or yellow skin; the tree bearing apples	75
approximate	(adjective) close to the actual; an estimate (verb) to come close or be similar to something	135
arch	(noun) a structure consisting of a curved top on two supports which holds the weight of something above it; the curved part of the bottom of the foot	87
archaeologist	(noun) a person who studies human history through the excavation of sites and the analysis of artifacts and other remains	111
architect	(noun) a person that designs buildings	111
arid	(adjective) very dry, having no rain	17, 70
armoire	(noun) a large wardrobe or cabinet	22
army	(noun) a military force; a large group	53, 100
aroma	(noun) a smell (usually pleasant); fragrance; odor	114
arrogant	(adjective) having an exaggerated sense of one's own importance or abilities	34, 38, 104
arsenal	(noun) a place where weapons and equipment are made or stored	53
ascend	(verb) to go up or climb; (noun – ascent)	49, 72, 73
ash	(noun) the soft, black powder left after something has burned; a tree that has a smooth gray bark	75
askew	(adjective) not straight or level	131, 132
aspect	(noun) a particular feature of or way of thinking about something	49
aspen	(noun) a tree of the poplar family	75
aspire	(verb) to want something very much; to hope to achieve something	49
assemble	(verb) to gather together in one place for a common purpose; to put together parts of a machine, furniture, or other object	85, 102
astute	(adjective) able to understand a situation quickly and how to take advantage of it	61
attainment	(noun) the act of achieving something toward a goal; achievement	63
attorney	(noun) a lawyer	111
audio	(adjective) of or involving sound; (noun) a sound recording; (root) hear	125, 127
auspicious	(adjective) suggesting a positive and successful future	24. 84, 96

Word	Definition	Seen on Pages
autobiography	(noun) a book written by a person about their own life	22
avarice	(noun) an extremely strong desire to obtain or keep wealth; greed	123
avoid	(verb) to stay away from someone or something; to prevent something from happening	70, 77
awkward	(adjective) difficult to use, or to deal with	24
axe	(noun) a tool used for cutting wood	41
axis	(noun) a straight line that goes through the center of an object that is spinning, or a line that divides a shape into two equal halves	41
baffle	(verb) to perplex or confuse	79, 95
baguette	(noun) a long, narrow French bread	85
baking	(noun) the process of cooking bread, cakes, etc. (adjective) very hot and dry	67
bald	(adjective) without hair on the head	43, 97
ball	(noun) a round object, used in many games; a sphere; a formal occasion where people dance; curved part of the foot that joins the big toe	8, 36, 87, 116, 127
balmy	(adjective) pleasantly warm	35, 67
banner	(noun) a long strip of cloth bearing a slogan or design; (adjective) excellent, outstanding	26
barometer	(noun) an instrument to measure air pressure	11
barrel	(noun) a large wooden container for liquid; the long part of a gun that is shaped like a tube; (verb) to move fast	53, 75
barren	(adjective) completely wanting or lacking; bleak, inhospitable; not bearing offspring	20
base	(noun) the bottom of an object; the place from which a business or person operates; a military area; (verb) to establish an area as the place from which a business or a person operates/works	41, 77
bashful	(adjective) shy	34
bass	(noun) a type of fish; the lowest part of the musical range; an instrument (guitar, etc)	22, 41
bassoon	(noun) a large musical instrument that is played by blowing into a long, curved tube	89
baste	(verb) to pour fat or meat juices on food while it cooks	41
bat	(noun) a wood or metal stick used in baseball or softball; a small, flying animal with big ears and wings of skin; (verb) to use a bat to hit a ball; to open and close your eyes quickly several times	9, 119
bawl	(verb) to cry or shout loudly	43, 97
beach	(noun) a flat, sloping area of sand or small stones beside the sea or a lake	9, 45
bear	(noun) a large, strong mammal with thick fur; (verb) to carry; to support; to accept; to have as a quality or characteristic; to produce	9, 117
bed	(noun) a place to sleep; the bottom of a river, lake, or sea; the ground used for planting flowers	53
beech	(noun) a tree with a smooth, gray trunk	45, 75
begonia	(noun) a type of plant with colorful flowers	22
belligerent	(adjective) eager to fight or argue	70
ben-	(root) good	125, 127
benefit	(verb) to be helped by something; (noun) a helpful or good effect; advantage	14
benign	(adjective) pleasant and kind; not harmful or severe	19
beret	(noun) a round, soft cap with no brim	22, 84
besiege	(verb) to surround a place with an army, to prevent people or supplies getting in or out; to be completely surrounded (besieged); to make many requests or complaints	56
betrayal	(noun) act of being disloyal	12
bewildered	(adjective) confused and uncertain	34
bi-	(root) two	125, 127
bilingual	(adjective) someone who can speak two languages fluently	32
bio-	(root) earth	125, 127
birch	(noun) a tree with a smooth, often white bark	75
biting	(adjective) weather that is extremely cold; severe and unpleasant; critical	67

Word	Definition	Seen on Pages
blacklist	(verb) to put someone's name on a list of people who are considered not acceptable; (noun) a list of names of people who have been considered unacceptable	56
blackmail	(noun) obtaining money by threat of exposing damaging information	8
blacksmith	(noun) someone who makes and repairs things in iron by hand	111
blank	(adjective) empty or clear, containing no information or mark; (noun) a form that has spaces to write in, or a space on a form	35, 64, 88, 107
blend	(verb) to mix together or combine; (noun) a mixture of different things	35, 77
bloated	(adjective) swollen from containing too much air, liquid, or food	82
boar	(noun) a male pig, or a type of wild pig	43
boastful	(adjective) exhibiting self-importance; bragging	20, 133
bolster	(verb) to support and strengthen	19, 70, 84
boot	(noun) a type of shoe that covers the foot and the lower leg; (verb) to kick something; to start up a computer	117
bore	(noun) someone who is not interesting; (verb) to make someone lose interest; to make a hole in something using a drilling tool	43
bough	(noun) a large branch of a tree	97
boundary	(noun) a real or imaginary line that marks the edge or limit of something; limit of a subject or principle	95
bountiful	(adjective) generous, abundant, ample	23
bouquet	(noun) an arrangement of flowers; a distinctive scent	114
boyhood	(noun) time of being a boy	8
buoyant	(adjective) able to float; happy and confident	11, 30
bovine	(adjective) of or related to cows	9, 26, 38
bow	(verb) to bend forward as a way of showing respect; (noun) the act of bowing; the front part of a ship; a knot used as a decoration or to tie shoes; a weapon for shooting arrows	87, 97, 119
brilliant	(adjective) extremely intelligent or skilled; very bright and full of light	96, 130
brisk	(adjective) active and energetic, quick	9
brisket	(noun) meat cut from the breast of an animal, usually beef or veal	9
brooch	(noun) jewelry worn with a pin to hold it in place	22
bulky	(adjective) large in size, particularly in proportion to its weight	9, 136
burden	(noun) a difficult duty or responsibility; a heavy load that you carry; (verb) to give someone problems, troubles or responsibilities	55
burdensome	(adjective) difficult to carry out or manage	9
bureau	(noun) a government office; a piece of furniture with drawers for keeping clothes	22
burgundy	(noun) a deep red color	9
cabana	(noun) a hut, cabin, or shelter at a beach or swimming pool	101
cacophony	(noun) a loud, harsh mixture of noises; noise, racket, din	11, 91, 114
calamity	(noun) an event causing great damage; disaster	134
callous	(adjective) unkind, cruel, and without sympathy or feeling for other people	35, 43, 123
callus	(noun) an area of hard, thick skin	43
camouflage	(noun) covering or clothing used to hide by blending into the background	35, 83, 134
candor	(noun) the quality of being honest and sincere	123
canine	(adjective) of or relating to dogs; (noun) a dog	26
capable	(adjective) having the skill or ability or strength to do something	84
capacity	(noun) the maximum amount that something can hold; the amount that something can produce	99
captive	(noun) a prisoner; (adjective, adverb) without being able to escape	72, 73
carbon	(noun) a chemical element that is contained in all animals and plants	51
caress	(verb) to touch or stroke gently; (noun) a gentle touch	114
cargo	(noun) goods carried by land, sea or air	51

Word	Definition	Seen on Pages
caricature	(noun) a drawing or picture of someone with exaggerated features	102
carp	(noun) a large fish that lives in lakes and rivers and can be eaten	36
carpenter	(noun) someone who makes and repairs wooden objects and structures	111
cartographer	(noun) a person who makes maps	111
case	(noun) a situation or example; arguments, facts, and reasons in support of or against something; a container	5, 8, 47, 113, 117
castanets	(noun) a musical instrument consisting of two small pieces of wood tied together by string and knocked against each other	89
casual	(adjective) relaxed, unconcerned; not regular or permanent	38, 102
catalog	(noun) a list of a collection of similar things	11
caution	(noun) a warning; careful attention; (verb) to warn someone	98
catastrophe	(noun) a sudden event that causes great suffering or destruction	56
cease	(verb) to stop an action or condition	17, 72, 73, 102
cent	(noun) unit of money worth 1/100th of a dollar	43
century	(noun) 100 years	9, 13
chaos	(noun) a state of disorder and confusion	14, 91
chaotic	(adjective) complete confusion and disorder	102
chaperone	(noun) a person that watches over and takes care of another, usually younger person	35, 56
charge	(verb) to ask a price for something; to buy something with credit; to accuse someone; to move forward quickly, attack; to store energy in a battery; (noun) responsibility for the control or care of something; storage of energy; an amount of explosives	107, 119
charmed	(adjective) unusually lucky or happy as though protected by magic	96
chastise	(verb) to scold, or criticize strongly	12, 17
chatter	(verb) to talk informally; (noun) informal talk	9, 97
cherished	(adjective) something that is loved, or cared for greatly	72, 73
cherry	(noun) small, soft round fruit, or the tree on which it grows	75
chide	(verb) to speak to someone severely because of bad behavior; lecture	35
chief	(adjective) most important; highest in position or power; (noun) the person in charge	85
chilly	(adjective) cold but not freezing	67
chisel	(noun) a tool with a long, metal blade that has a sharp edge for cutting or shaping wood, stone, or metal	63, 85, 89, 113
chord	(noun) three or more musical notes played at a time	43, 61
chromo-	(root) color	125, 127
chute	(noun) a narrow, steep slope down which objects or people can slide	45
circulate	(verb) to move around or through; to send something such as information or ideas, from one person to another	112
civil	(adjective) of or relating to the ordinary people of a country, rather than religious groups or the military; polite and formal	35
clarify	(verb) to make something clear or easy to understand	56, 84
cleats	(noun) athletic shoes	22
cloak	(noun) a piece of clothing without sleeves that fastens at the neck and hangs from the shoulders; something that hides another thing; (verb) to cover or hide something	83
close	(adjective) nearby; (verb) to shut; to cause something to end	47, 85
clutch	(verb) to hold on to something tightly; (noun) part of a car you press down to change gears; a group of eggs or young animals hatched from eggs; a small bag with no handle or strap	53
coarse	(adjective) rough, not smooth or soft; rude in manner of speech	55, 81, 91

Word	Definition	Seen on Pages
coax	(verb) to gently persuade	14
cod	(noun) a type of large sea fish	22
colonel	(noun) a high military rank	97
commence	(verb) to begin	37, 83
commend	(verb) to formally praise	12, 19
common	(adjective) found or occurring frequently; shared by two or more people; an area of land that is open for everyone to use	70, 81, 124, 133
compass	(noun) an instrument for measuring direction	55
compassion	(noun) a strong feeling of sympathy for other's suffering or sadness and a desire to help	91
compel	(verb) to force someone to do something	81
complete	(adjective) whole; containing everything; (verb) to finish; to make whole	63, 85, 89, 113
comprehensive	(adjective) complete; including everything that is necessary	83
conceal	(verb) to prevent something from being seen or known about; to hide something	38, 83, 104, 123, 138
concede	(verb) to admit that something is true; to admit you have lost	133
conceited	(adjective) excessively proud of oneself; vain	34
conclusion	(noun) the ending or finish of an event, process or text; the decision reached by reasoning	138
concur	(verb) to agree; to happen at the same time	9, 91
condemn	(verb) to criticize something or someone strongly; to severely punish; to declare a building unsafe	55
condiment	(noun) substance such as a spice used to enhance a food's flavor	55
confidential	(adjective) intended to be kept secret; private	82
conflict	(noun) a serious disagreement; dispute (verb) to be incompatible; to clash	135
confound	(verb) to cause surprise or confusion	80, 134
confront	(verb) to deal with a difficult problem, situation, or person	70, 133
conscious	(adjective) aware of one's surroundings; having knowledge of something	34
consequence	(noun) a result of an action or situation, that is usually bad; the condition of having a lasting effect	133
consideration	(noun) caring about or respecting something; thinking about something carefully	99
console	(verb) to give comfort and sympathy; (noun) a panel or unit containing a set of controls for electronic or mechanical equipment	47, 119
conspicuous	(adjective) clearly visible; attracting notice or attention	134
constant	(adjective) unchanging; nearly continuous or very frequent	35, 79, 84
constrict	(verb) to make or become tighter and narrower	105
contact	(verb) to touch; to be in communication with	85, 113-14
contemporary	(adjective) existing or happening now; (noun) someone living during the same period as another; a person the same age as you	55, 77
content	(adjective) to be pleased; (noun) the subject or ideas contained in something; the amount of a particular substance contained	47
contest	(noun) a competition; (verb) to oppose in an argument; to claim that something is unfair or against the rules	47
contract	(noun) a written agreement; (verb) to become smaller, decrease in size	85
contraction	(noun) the process of becoming smaller; when a muscle is made tighter	13, 138
contradict	(verb) to state the opposite of what someone else has said	109, 135
conundrum	(noun) a difficult problem that is hard to solve	95
copious	(adjective) in large amounts; more than enough	55
copse	(noun) a small group of trees	97
copyright	(noun) a legal right that protects work from being copied	11

Word	Definition	Seen on Pages
cord	(noun) a rope; length of string or wire	43
cordial	(adjective) friendly or pleasant; (noun) a strongly-flavored sweet drink	19
corresponding	(adjective) similar or the same in some way	16, 24
cosmetologist	(noun) a person who gives beauty treatments	111
counter	(noun) a long, flat, narrow surface at which people are served; (verb) to react to something with an opposing opinion or action; to defend yourself	117
courageous	(adjective) brave, not deterred by danger or pain	32
cover	(verb) to put or spread something over another thing; to travel a particular distance; to include something; to report or write about a particular subject; to be enough; to protect or insure; to do a job or take care of something for someone else; (noun) shelter or protection; something that is placed over something else	14, 38, 83, 119
cowardly	(adjective) lacking courage	70
coy	(adjective) acting shy, uncertain, or unwilling to say much	25, 61
cranium	(noun) the top portion of the skull, which protects the brain	63
cravat	(noun) a wide, straight piece of material worn loosely tied in the open neck of a shirt	22, 85
craving	(noun) a strong feeling of wanting something, usually food	96, 136
creek	(noun) a small stream	26
crochet	(noun) a type of knitting; clothes or other things made with crochet	56
crucial	(adjective) decisive or critical in the success of something	9
cruel	(adjective) extremely unkind and intentionally causing pain	18, 77
cue	(noun) a signal or prompt to do something; long stick used in pool or billiards	97
cufflinks	(noun) jewelry used to fasten the cuffs of a shirt	22
cunning	(adjective) skillful in planning, especially through deception	69, 96
cymbals	(noun - plural) a flat, round metal instrument hit with a stick or struck against another such instrument to make a loud noise	45, 89
daisy	(noun) a type of flower	22
dawdle	(verb) to waste time, be slow	9
dash	(verb) to move quickly; to hit with great force, causing damage; (noun) a small amount of something added to or mixed with something else; a short, horizontal mark (–); the act of running somewhere quickly; a short race	117
dawn	(noun) beginning of daylight before sunrise	12
dearth	(noun) a scarcity or lack of something	12, 56
debate	(noun) a formal discussion; (verb) to discuss a subject in a formal way; to try to make a decision about something	77
debrief	(verb) to question someone in detail about work they have done for you	61
decade	(noun) ten years	9, 13
decay	(verb) to rot or decompose; to become gradually damaged, or worse; (noun) damage, or a state that becomes gradually worse	102
deceitful	(adjective) untrustworthy, misleading, keeping the truth hidden	12, 34, 91
deceive	(verb) to persuade someone to believe something that is not true; lie	133
deceptive	(adjective) misleading	34. 57
decline	(verb) to go down in amount or quality, lessen; to refuse something	17, 47
decorate	(verb) to add something to an object or place in order to make it more attractive; to honor a person by giving him or her a medal or badge	134
deflated	(adjective) having been emptied of air or gas; having lost confidence or optimism	82
defile	(verb) to damage the appearance or purity of something	98
defy	(verb) to refuse to obey	109
dejected	(adjective) sad, dispirited	32
delayed	(adjective) late; happening at a later time than expected or intended	77, 102, 107
deliberation	(noun) long and careful consideration; slow and careful movement or thought	98

Word	Definition	Seen on Pages
delusion	(noun) belief in something that is not true	95
demeanor	(noun) a way of looking and behaving	56
demolish	(verb) to completely destroy	55, 85
dense	(adjective) close together; thick	43
depressed	(adjective) a state of unhappiness	32
deprive	(verb) to take something away or prevent someone from having something that is usually necessary or pleasant	38
desert	(noun) a waterless, desolate area of land with little or no vegetation; (verb) to abandon; to leave; to illegally leave the military	97
dessert	(noun) the sweet course eaten at the end of the meal	97
despondent	(adjective) in low spirits from loss of hope or courage	32
despot	(noun) a ruler who has unlimited power, and uses it unfairly	91
detect	(verb) to discover or identify something; observe; uncover	95, 114
devious	(adjective) to use dishonest methods to get something; to use indirect ways	55
dice	(noun) two small cubes with dots used in many games; to cut food into small squares	97
die	(noun) a single cube with dots from a set of dice; (verb) to stop living	18, 60, 97
dietician	(noun) an expert on diet and nutrition	111
diligent	(adjective) done in a careful and determined way	34, 69
dilute	(verb) to make a liquid weaker by mixing in something else	56
din	(noun) a loud, unpleasant confused noise that lasts for a long time	61
dinghy	(noun) a small boat	26
diplomatic	(adjective) careful not to offend; achieving peaceful resolutions by not taking sides	9
dire	(adjective) very serious or extreme	56
discourage	(verb) to cause someone to lose confidence or enthusiasm to do something; to prevent something from happening	70. 82, 84
discuss	(verb) to talk about something; exchange ideas	85
disfigure	(verb) to spoil the appearance of something	98
disheveled	(adjective) untidy, disordered	136
dishearten	(verb) to make someone lose confidence or hope	13
disobey	(verb) to refuse to do something that you are told to do	35
dispel	(verb) to remove fears, doubts, or false ideas	25
dispute	(noun) an argument	63
dissipate	(verb) to disappear gradually	25, 56
distraught	(adjective) very worried and upset	12
distinct	(adjective) visibly different from something else of a similar type; unmistakable	104
dither	(verb) to be unable to make a decision about doing something	17
diversity	(noun) variety; being composed of differing elements or qualities	134
dogwood	(noun) a bush or tree that has white or pink flowers in the spring	75
donate	(verb) to give money or goods to help someone	77
donation	(noun) money or goods that are given to help a person or organization	61
drastic	(adjective) severe and sudden; extreme	70, 138
dromedary	(noun) an Arabian camel with one hump	26
drowsy	(adjective) sleepy	70
dual	(adjective) consisting of two parts	97
dubious	(adjective) probably not true; not to be trusted	24
duck	(noun) a bird that lives by water and has short legs with webbed feet; (verb) to move your head down to avoid being hit; to move quickly to a place in order not to be seen	8, 36, 117
duel	(noun) a fight between two people to settle a point of honor	9, 97
duo	(noun) a pair of people or things	9
dusk	(noun) the time before night when it is not yet dark	12

Word	Definition	Seen on Pages
dwelling	(noun) a place where people live	85, 95
dwindle	(verb) to become less in number or smaller	100
eavesdrop	(verb) to secretly listen to a conversation	114
ebb	(noun) the movement of the tide out to sea; (verb) to move away from the land; recede; to gradually decrease	102
ebony	(noun) black	14
echo	(noun) a sound that is heard again after it has been reflected off a surface; (verb) to fill a place with repeating sounds; to say or think what someone else has already said	38
economize	(verb) to spend less	102
economy	(noun) the careful use of money and resources; the system of how money is made and used within a particular country or region; economical (adjective) – careful with resources	111, 136
effort	(noun) physical or mental work needed to achieve something; a serious attempt	63
effortless	(adjective) easy, requiring no effort; achieved with ease	135
elaborate	(adjective) containing a lot of complicated details; (verb) to give more information or explain something further	134
elderly	(adjective) old; (noun) old people considered as a group	85
elephantine	(adjective) of, or relating to an elephant	9
elevated	(adjective) raised; high or important	63, 134
elm	(noun) a large tree valued for the shade it provides	75
embark	(verb) to go on to a ship or an aircraft; to begin a course of action	105
embellish	(verb) to decorate, make beautiful with ornamentation; exaggerate	136
embezzled	(adjective) stolen money, from one's own workplace	102
emigrate	(verb) to leave one's own country in order to settle permanently in another	38
emphasize	(verb) to state or show that something is especially important	105
enchanting	(adjective) appealing; charming; delightful	136
enclosure	(noun) an area surrounded by a fence or wall; something extra added to a letter	95
encyclopedia	(noun) a reference work containing articles on various topics	22
endanger	(adjective) in danger of being lost, harmed or hurt	12, 49
endure	(verb) to suffer something difficult or painful	49
engineer	(noun) someone trained to design and build machines, structures, systems, etc.; someone who drives a train; (verb) to plan, design, or build something	111
enigma	(noun) someone or something that is mysterious and impossible to understand	91
enlighten	(verb) to give someone greater knowledge about a subject or situation	80
enormous	(adjective) extremely large	61, 73
equine	(adjective) related to horses	9
equivalent	(adjective) equal in value, amount, function, etc.	135
eradicate	(verb) to eliminate; completely destroy	135, 138
erratic	(adjective) changing suddenly and unexpectedly	84
escalate	(verb) to become greater or more serious	55, 91
essay	(noun) a short piece of writing on a particular subject	63
establish	(verb) to start or create something (company, organization, etc.); to cause something to be accepted; to prove something	70
esteem	(noun) respect or high regard for someone; (verb) to respect someone, admire	38, 104, 135
ewe	(noun) a female sheep	43
exaggerate	(verb) to represent something as larger, better, or worse than it is	13, 112, 136
exasperated	(adjective) extremely irritated and frustrated	32
excavate	(verb) to dig a hole in the ground; to dig in order to find old objects buried underneath	38
excessive	(adjective) more than is necessary; too much	96
exhale	(verb) to breathe out air	91

Word	Definition	Seen on Pages
exhaust	(verb) to make someone feel tired; to use up completely; (noun) waste gas expelled from an engine	70, 135
exhaustive	(adjective) detailed and complete	83
exhibit	(verb) to publicly display something at a gallery, museum, fair, etc.; to reveal or display; (noun) something on display at a gallery, museum, fair. Etc.	105
exhilarating	(adjective) making one feel very happy and excited, thrilled	95
exorbitant	(adjective) unreasonably high-priced; excessive	96
expand	(verb) to increase in size, number or importance; become bigger	60
expansion	(noun) the action of becoming larger; a thing formed by the enlargement of something	13, 138
expel	(verb) to force someone to leave a country, organization, or school	63
expenditure	(noun) an amount of money, time, or effort that is spent	55
explicit	(adjective) clear and exact; giving full details	130, 132
exposition	(noun) a statement that explains something clearly; a big public event in which the goods of many different companies or organizations are shown	134
exquisite	(adjective) especially beautiful or admirable	72, 73
exterior	(adjective) relating to the outside of something; (noun) the outer surface or structure of something	102
extinct	(adjective) not now existing	11
extract	(verb) to remove or take out something; (noun) a small part of a book that is published separately; substance	91
extravagant	(adjective) spending too much money; expensive; exceeding what is reasonable	96
excuse	(verb) to forgive someone; (noun) the explanation given for bad behavior, absence, etc.	47
fabrication	(noun) the act of inventing false information in order to deceive; a lie; the act of producing a product	56
facetious	(adjective) not being serious, to make someone laugh or to trick them	24
faint	(verb) to become unconscious unexpectedly for a short time; 9adjective) not strong or clear; slight; very weak and nearly becoming unconscious	63, 131
fair	(adjective) treating someone in a way that is right or reasonable; average, neither good nor bad; large or great in comparison; correct; pale; a public event, usually held outside, where goods and sometimes farm animals are shown	119
fake	(noun) not genuine, a copy; (verb) to pretend	61, 70
falter	(verb) to lose strength or purpose and pause or stop; to lose confidence	56
familiar	(adjective) easily recognizable; known; informal or friendly	70, 82
famished	(adjective) very hungry	96
fantasy	(noun) something pleasant that you imagine, that is not real; imaginative literature	95, 138
farrier	(noun) a person that makes and fits shoes for horses	111
fatal	(adjective) causing death; very serious and having an important bad effect	105, 112
fathom	(noun) a unit of measurement of the depth of water (6 feet); (verb) to understand	55
fawning	(adjective) praising someone too much, flattering	25
feeble	(adjective) weak, lacking strength	13, 32
feat	(noun) an act that shows skill, strength, or bravery	97
feline	(adjective) of or related to cats	9, 26
ferment	(verb) to change chemically through the action of living substances, like yeast or bacteria; incite or cause trouble	56
ferocious	(adjective) fierce, cruel, or violent	14, 107
fertile	(adjective) capable of reproducing; prolific; fruitful	19
festive	(adjective) cheerful and merry; relating to a festival	32
fickle	(adjective) not consistent; subject to change	136
fiction	(noun) a type of book or story that is written about imaginary characters and events	109
fierce	(adjective) violent and forceful, extremely strong	14, 91
fig	(noun) a tree that grows in warm places; the soft, sweet fruit of the fig tree	36

Word	Definition	Seen on Pages
fir	(noun) a tall evergreen tree	75
firm	(adjective, adverb) set in place and unable or unlikely to move; (adjective) not soft when pressed; solid or strong; certain or fixed in a belief or opinion; (noun) a business	117
flaw	(noun) a fault or weakness	105
flawless	(adjective) containing no faults or mistakes; perfect	55, 123
flee	(verb) to escape by running away	97
flex	(verb) to bend a part of the body; to tighten a muscle	35
flippant	(adjective) not serious, attempting to be funny or clever	91
flotilla	(noun) a fleet of ships	9, 26
foe	(noun) an enemy, or a competitor	63, 109
foil	(noun) a very thin sheet of metal, used for wrapping food; a blade used in fencing; someone who in comparison makes good qualities noticeable; (verb) to prevent something from happening	63, 119
foliage	(noun) leaves of a plant collectively	26, 56
foolish	(adjective) stupid; unwise	138
forceps	(noun) an instrument with two handles used in medical operations for picking up, pulling, and holding things	89
foreboding	(noun) the feeling that something bad is going to happen	24
forethought	(noun) careful consideration of something that might happen, anticipation	8
forgo	(verb) to give up or do without	55
formidable	(adjective) impressively large, powerful, intense, or capable; intimidating	13
fortify	(verb) to make something stronger, in order to protect it	138
fortitude	(noun) bravery when dealing with pain or difficulty, especially over a long period	112
fortress	(noun) a large, strong building; a military stronghold	26
fortuitous	(adjective) happening by lucky chance, rather than intention	96
fortunate	(adjective) lucky	96, 102, 138
foul	(adjective) extremely unpleasant; (noun) an act that is against the rules	38, 41
foundry	(noun) a factory (for casting metal)	26
foundation	(noun) the base that supports a building; the act of establishing an organization, state, etc.; an organization that provides financial support for activities and groups	77
fowl	(noun) a bird that is used to produce meat or eggs	41
fragrant	(adjective) having a sweet, or pleasant smell	114
frail	(adjective) weak and delicate	32, 82
framework	(noun) a structure around or over which something is built; a system of rules, ideas, or beliefs that is used to plan or decide something	130, 132
freezing	(noun) the change from a liquid to solid; (adjective) cold enough for water to turn to ice	67
frequent	(adjective) often; (verb) to visit a place often	102
fret	(verb) to worry or be unhappy	77, 107
frigid	(adjective) extremely cold	67
frosty	(adjective) very cold, with frost forming on surfaces; cold and unfriendly	67
furious	(adjective) very angry, upset	32, 72, 73
futile	(adjective) not effective or successful; having no effect; achieving nothing	55
gait	(noun) a way of walking	45
gallant	(adjective) brave, heroic	32, 38, 134
gargantuan	(adjective) very large; huge	56
gauntlet	(noun) a long, thick glove	35, 56
gavel	(noun) a small hammer used by a judge to call a court to order	55
gem	(noun) a precious stone; something valued due to quality or beauty	72, 73

Word	Definition	Seen on Pages
genes	(noun) cells passed down through generations	43
genius	(noun) very great and rare natural ability or skill	34
gent	(noun) informal for gentleman	104
gentle	(adjective) calm, soft or kind	38, 60, 138
genuine	(adjective) real; honest; sincere	61, 70, 84
geo-	(root) earth	125, 127
gifted	(adjective) having a special ability; intelligent or having a great range of abilities	34, 96
gigantic	(adjective) extremely large	138
gingerly	(adverb) in a slow, cautious or careful way	72, 73
gist	(noun) the main subject, without details	91
glade	(noun) a small area of grass without trees in a forest	37
glazier	(noun) someone who fits glass into windows and doors	111
glistening	(adjective) shining brightly	73
glutton	(noun) a person who regularly eats too much	91
goggles	(noun) special glasses worn to protect the eyes	22
gown	(noun) a long dress worn on formal occasions	22, 55
grant	(verb) to give something as an official act; to accept that something is true; (noun) an amount of money that is given by a government or organization for a special purpose	100, 119
grasp	(verb) to hold something firmly; to understand; (noun) power to achieve or control something	36, 87
grave	(noun) a place where a dead person is buried; (adjective) urgent and very bad; serious	37, 109
graze	(verb) (of an animal) to eat grass in a field; (informal) to snack on something	114
gregarious	(adjective) liking to be with other people; outgoing	61, 123
grimace	(noun) an expression of pain or disgust, in which the face twists in an ugly way	61
gripe	(verb) to complain; (noun) a complaint	136
grotesque	(adjective) strange and often frightening in appearance or character; ugly	14
gruesome	(adjective) extremely unpleasant and shocking, usually dealing with death or injury	55
guarantee	(verb) to promise with certainty; (noun) a formal promise from a company regarding performance of a product or service; a promise	102
guise	(noun) the appearance of someone or something	41, 91
gullible	(adjective) easily persuaded to believe something; over-trusting	102
habitat	(noun) the natural home or environment of an animal, plant, or other organism	38
haddock	(noun) a type of sea fish	22, 26
hapless	(adjective) unlucky; unfortunate	17, 105, 138
harmony	(noun) the combination of musical notes to produce a pleasing effect; an agreement of ideas, feelings, or actions	70
hark	(verb) listen	114
harp	(noun) a large, triangle-shaped string instrument; (verb) to repeat or complain about something many times in an annoying way	9, 36, 97
hart	(noun) a male deer	37
haughty	(adjective) arrogantly superior, vain	34
headdress	(noun) an ornamental covering for the head, usually worn for a special occasion	8
heir	(noun) a person in line to receive an estate or other fortune when the other person dies; someone who continues to do the work of someone important who has died	61
helix	(noun) a spiral shape	26
herd	(noun) a large group of animals of the same type; (verb) to move together as a group	36
hereditary	(adjective) passed from the genes of a parent to a child (disease or condition); passed from parent to a child as a right (title, society position)	112
heroic	(adjective) very brave or great	38, 70, 134
hesitate	(verb) to pause before saying or doing something; to be reluctant to do something	18, 104
hickory	(noun) a North American tree of the walnut family	75

Word	Definition	Seen on Pages
hinder	(verb) to delay, obstruct, make it difficult for something to happen	18, 107
hindrance	(noun) something that provides resistance; an obstruction	138
hoard	(verb) to collect a large supply of something, and hide it away; (noun) a large amount of something that someone has saved and hidden	69
hoarse	(adjective) having a rough voice (usually with a sore throat)	41
hoax	(noun) a plan to deceive; a trick; (verb) to trick or deceive	38, 84
horde	(noun) a very large, unorganized group of people	87
horizon	(noun) the place in the distance where the earth and sky seem to meet	99
horizontal	(adjective) flat or level; parallel with the ground	70
host	(noun) someone who gives a party or has guests; a large number; a plant or animal that another plant or animal lives on as a parasite; (verb) to be the host for guests	9, 53
hub	(noun) the central part of something; the center of activity	76, 84
humble	(adjective) modest, unassuming	14, 19
humid	(adjective) hot weather containing extremely small drops of water in the air	67
hutch	(noun) a piece of furniture used for storing or showing dishes	15
hydrant	(noun) a fitting in a public place that supplies water (fire hydrant)	22
hyper-	(root) over	125, 127
hypo-	(root) under	125, 127
icon	(noun) a well-known person or thing that represents something of importance; a symbol that starts a program or feature on a computer or smartphone; a painting of a religious figure	38, 60
icy	(adjective) extremely cold; covered with ice; unfriendly and showing dislike	67
idle	(adjective) not working, not active, or doing nothing; (verb) an engine that is operating but not doing any work	61, 84, 139
igloo	(noun) a circular house made of blocks of hard snow	9
ignite	(verb) to start burning or explode; to cause a dangerous situation to begin	72, 73
ignore	(verb) to give no attention to someone or something	82
illegal	(adjective) against the law	35, 60
illegible	(adjective) impossible or difficult to read because it is unclear	91
illuminate	(verb) to put light in or on something; to explain and show more clearly	130, 132
immense	(adjective) extremely large or great	102
immerse	(verb) to involve someone completely in an activity; to put something completely under the surface of a liquid	61
immigrate	(verb) to come to live in a different country	91
imp	(noun) a small, devilish creature	26
impair	(verb) to damage or weaken something, so that it is less effective	89
impatient	(adjective) unprepared to wait, restless, anxious	9
impeccable	(adjective) perfect; without fault	123
impede	(verb) to slow something down; to make it more difficult for something to happen	55
impertinent	(adjective) rude; not restrained; audacious	136
imply	(verb) to suggest something without saying it directly	91
import	(verb) to bring in products or goods from another country for sale or use; (noun) the importance given to something; a product that has been imported	61
impractical	(adjective) not effective or reasonable	13, 138
impure	(adjective) mixed with foreign matter; immoral	80
incessantly	(adverb) never stopping	69
incision	(noun) a cut made in the skin or in other body tissue	37, 85
incite	(verb) to encourage someone to do or feel something unpleasant or violent	123
inclement	(adjective) unpleasant, especially cold or stormy	67
incognito	(adverb) avoiding being recognized, by changing your name or appearance	99, 105

Word	Definition	Seen on Pages
index	(noun) an alphabetical list; a number used to show the value of something by comparison; name for the first finger next to the thumb; (verb) to arrange information in an list for a book, etc.	53
indifferent	(adjective) not interested; not concerned	136
indigo	(noun) a dark blue color	9
indistinct	(adjective) not clear	131, 132
indolent	(adjective) lazy; without real interest or effort	34
indulge	(verb) to allow yourself or another person to have something enjoyable; to treat	51
industrious	(adjective) hard-working	34, 55
inferior	(adjective) not as good as others of the same type; of a lower rank	138
inferno	(noun) a large uncontrolled fire	49
inflexible	(adjective) unwilling to change; not able to be bent	72, 73
influence	(verb) to cause something to be changed; to change people's opinion, behavior or beliefs; (noun) the power to change people's opinion, behavior or beliefs	56, 113
ingratiating	(adjective) behavior intended to make people like you	24
inoculate	(verb) to treat with a vaccine	11
inquire	(verb) to ask for information	109
inscribe	(verb) to write words in a book or carve words onto the surface of an object	51
insolent	(adjective) intentionally and rudely showing no respect	138
insure	(verb) to make something certain, or to be certain about something; to buy insurance	51
intercept	(verb) to stop things, people, etc. as they go to a particular place	109
interminable	(adjective) seeming never to end	131, 132
internal	(adjective) inside	109
interpreter	(noun) a person who translates speech orally or into sign language	32
interrogate	(verb) to ask questions formally, in a forceful or threatening way	87
interval	(noun) a period between two events or times, or the space between two points; an intermission	77
intrigue	(verb) to arouse the curiosity or interest of someone; (noun) the making of a secret plan	99
invalid	(adjective) not true or acceptable; (noun) a person who is ill or injured for a long time and usually has to be cared for by others	47
irate	(adjective) feeling great anger, furious	32, 69
ire	(noun) anger	38
irrigate	(verb) to supply land with water; to wash part of an injured person's body with a liquid	14
irritated	(adjective) annoyed	69
jam	(verb) to pack tightly into a small space; to become stuck and unable to move; to play popular music informally with other people; (noun) a difficult situation; a soft, sweet food made by cooking fruit with sugar	117
jeans	(noun) pants made of denim	43, 103
jeer	(verb) to laugh at or shout insults at someone; to ridicule	56
jester	(noun) a joker; in medieval times paid to make people laugh	14
jewelry	(noun) an adornment (such as a ring, necklace, etc) worn by a person	23
jigsaw	(noun) a picture puzzle that is put together by joining pieces; an electric saw with a thin metal blade that is used for cutting curves in flat materials, such as wood or metal	89
John Doe	(noun) name given to an unknown person	99
jovial	(adjective) cheerful and friendly	32
juniper	(noun) an evergreen shrub or small tree that bears berrylike cones	75
kernel	(noun) the edible (inside part) of a nut; seed of a grain	97
key	(noun) the metal piece that opens a lock; an important part; a movable part (of a computer, piano, etc); musical notes; a list of symbols; (adjective) very important and having a lot of influence on other people or things	8, 9, 119

Word	Definition	Seen on Pages
kin	(noun) family; relatives	109
kindle	(verb) to start a fire burning; to cause strong feelings in someone	61
knead	(verb) to press something firmly with the hands (usually bread dough); massage	43
labyrinth	(noun) a confusing set of connecting passages in which it is easy to get lost; a maze	77, 107
lack	(verb) to be without; (noun) a condition of not having any or enough of something	38, 41
lament	(verb) to express sadness and regret over something; (noun) an expression of sadness or regret; a complaint	38
lap	(noun) the surface of the upper part of the legs of a person who is sitting down; one complete trip around a race track or pool; (verb) to make one complete trip around a track; (of an animal) to drink a liquid; (of waves) to hit something gently	9, 117
lark	(noun) a small, brown bird; an activity done as an amusement	63
latitude	(noun) the distance north or south of the equator measured from 0° to 90°; freedom to behave, act, or think in the way you want to	99, 112
launch	(verb) to send something out; (noun) an introduction of a new plan or product; a motor boat; the act of sending something out	35, 83
lavish	(adjective) spending, giving, or using more than is necessary or reasonable	14
lax	(adjective) casual, lacking care; not severe or strong enough	41, 123
lecturer	(noun) someone who teaches at a college or university	98
leek	(noun) a vegetable from the onion family	41
leisurely	(adjective) relaxed, easy-going	9
lenient	(adjective) not as severe in punishment or judgment as would be expected	123
leotard	(noun) stretchy clothing used by dancers and for exercise	9
lethal	(adjective) deadly	57
lethargic	(adjective) lacking in energy; slow moving	34, 61
lethargy	(noun) having little energy and being unwilling or unable to do anything	139
lexicon	(noun) a dictionary; all the words used in a particular language or subject	105
liable	(adjective) likely to do or happen; to be legally responsible	55
limb	(noun) an arm, leg or a wing; a large branch of a tree	61, 85, 112
limit	(noun) the greatest amount allowed or possible; (verb) to control something so that it is not greater than a particular amount, number, or level	80
litter	(noun) trash left in public places; a group of baby animals; (verb) to throw trash on the ground in public places	53
livid	(adjective) very angry	55
lob	(verb) to throw something, usually in a high arc	38
locket	(noun) a small item of jewelry often worn around the neck	22
lodge	(verb) to become fixed or cause something to become fixed in a place or position; to stay in a place temporarily; (noun) a small building used during a sports season; a type of hotel in the countryside or mountains	60
lodging	(noun) a temporary place to stay	95
lofty	(adjective) of imposing height, tall	13, 91
logo	(noun) a design that a company or organization uses as its symbol; (root) word; reason	125, 127
loot	(noun) money or valuables, that have usually been stolen; (verb) to steal	40
loyalty	(noun) a strong feeling of support or duty toward a person or cause	12
lucid	(adjective) expressed clearly, easy to understand; bright or luminous	9, 69
ludicrous	(adjective) foolish, unreasonable	32
lukewarm	(adjective) only slightly warm; unenthusiastic (reaction)	67
lute	(noun) a string instrument, with a pear-shaped body and an angled neck	40
luxurious	(adjective) comfortable and expensive	14
mace	(noun) a club like weapon; a chemical spray used in self-defense	26

Word	Definition	Seen on Pages
magnolia	(noun) a tree or shrub with large pink or white flowers	75
maim	(verb) to injure someone severely	55
maize	(noun) corn	55, 85
major	(adjective) of great importance; (noun) a military rank; an area of study in college or university	107
mal-	(root) bad	125, 127
malady	(noun) a disease, or a problem in the way something works	17, 61
malicious	(adjective) unkind, cruel	17, 34
manor	(noun) a large house with land belonging to it	26
mantel	(noun) a shelf above a fireplace	130-132
maple	(noun) a type of large tree that is valued for its timber as well as its syrup	75
mar	(verb) to spoil or damage something, making it less attractive or enjoyable	38
martyr	(noun) a person who suffers and is killed, because of political or religious beliefs; (verb) to be killed, because of political or religious beliefs	60, 91
mask	(noun) a covering for all or part of the face; (verb) to prevent something from being seen or noticed	83
massive	(adjective) very large in size	70
match	(verb) to be similar to or the same as something; to combine well with something or someone else; (noun) a sports competition or event; a short stick that ignites to create a flame;	121
mayhem	(noun) confused activity or excitement	14
meager	(adjective) very small in amount or number, usually not sufficient	38
meander	(verb) to follow a route that bends or twists	72, 73
mechanism	(noun) a part of a machine, or a set of parts that work together; a system	130, 132
menacing	(adjective) threatening	24
mend	(verb) to repair. fix	9, 35
mentally	(noun) in the mind; regarding one's mind	11
mere	(adjective) used to emphasize that something is not large or important	76, 113
methodical	(adjective) well organized, well thought out, orderly	9, 91
mild	(adjective) slight or gentle; not very cold or not as cold as usual	38, 67, 70
millennium	(noun) one thousand years	9
mingle	(verb) to mix; to be with and among other people	69
minor	(adjective) not great in size or importance; (noun) a young person who is not yet an adult; the second most important subject that a college student is studying	107
minuscule	(adjective) extremely small	138
mirth	(noun) amusement and laughter	55
misleading	(adjective) causing someone to believe something that is not true	34
mobile	(noun) able to move easily, or to be easily moved; a decoration that is hung by a string, usually over a baby's crib; (adjective) moving or walking around freely; used to describe a service available on a mobile phone, tablet computer, etc.	139
modern	(adjective) of the present; using recently developed ideas, methods, or styles; up-to-date	77, 107
modest	(adjective) humble; not large in size, or not great in value	14, 63
modify	(verb) to change something, in order to improve it or make it more acceptable	99
moisture	(noun) small drops of water in the air or on a surface	96
moral	(adjective) relating to standards of good behavior, honesty, and fair dealing; behaving in ways considered to be correct and honest; (noun) a message about how people should behave, contained in a story, event, or experience	61
morbid	(adjective) too interested in unpleasant subjects, especially death	112
morose	(adjective) unhappy, sad, ill-tempered	104

Word	Definition	Seen on Pages
morph	(verb) to change gradually in appearance or form, from one thing to another	99
mortician	(noun) a funeral director, oversees funeral arrangements	111
mourning	(noun) a time of grief following the death of a loved one	45
murder	(noun) the crime of intentionally killing someone; a group of crows; (verb) to intentionally kill someone	53
myriad	(noun) a very large number, countless	35
mystify	(verb) to confuse by being or doing something very strange or impossible to explain	134
nadir	(noun) the lowest or least successful point; the worst moment	12, 20
nail	(noun) metal pins used in carpentry; the hard part at the upper end of each finger and toe; (verb) to attach or fasten with a nail or nails	85, 119
naive	(adjective) showing a lack of experience, wisdom, or judgement	79
nauseous	(adjective) a feeling that you are going to be sick	55
neon	(noun) a colorless gas, one of the chemical elements, that is often used in signs because it produces a bright light when an electric current goes through it	61
nest	(noun) a place where animals give birth or leave their eggs to develop; a comfortable home; (verb) to build a nest, or live in a nest	9, 53
nimble	(adjective) quick and light in movement; agile	32, 35 77, 107
noble	(adjective) having or showing high moral qualities or character; having a high social rank from birth; (noun) a person of high social rank from birth	63
nod	(verb) to move your head up and down, to show agreement or approval; to let your head fall forward when going to sleep	38
nonchalant	(adjective) behaving in a calm, care-free manner	38
nonentity	(noun) a person or thing of no importance	56
notice	(verb) to become aware of; (noun) something written or printed that gives information or instructions; attention	81, 131
novice	(noun) a beginner; someone without any experience	56, 136
nylon	(noun) an artificial substance used to make clothing, brushes, etc.	84
oak	(noun) a large tree which bears acorns and is an important source of timber used in building and furniture	75
oasis	(noun) a fertile spot in a desert, where water is found	55, 107
oath	(noun) an official promise that you will tell the truth, or will do what you have said	61
obedient	(adjective) willing to do what you have been told to do	70, 138
object	(noun) a thing; the purpose of an activity; the person or thing to which an action or feeling is directed; (verb) to disapprove, dislike	47, 111, 121
oblige	(verb) to force or make it expected for someone to do something; to please or help someone	82
obscure	(adjective) not known to many people; unclear or difficult to understand; (verb) to prevent something from being seen or heard, or being discovered	70, 84 85
obvious	(adjective) easily understood; clear, self-evident	38, 85, 102
ominous	(adjective) suggesting something unpleasant will happen; threatening	84
omit	(verb) to fail to include or do something	60, 63 70
onerous	(adjective) causing great difficulty or needing a lot of effort	35
opaque	(adjective) not letting light through and therefore being able to see through it	56, 136
oppress	(verb) to keep someone in subjection and hardship, by the unjust use of authority	138
optimal	(adjective) being the best or most likely to bring success	63
optimistic	(adjective) hoping or believing that good things will happen in the future	11, 56
orchestra	(noun) a large group of musicians led by a conductor	53

Word	Definition	Seen on Pages
origin	(noun) the beginning, or start of something	14, 91, 138
original	(adjective) existing since the beginning, not a copy	12
originate	(verb) to come from or begin in a particular place or situation	84
orthodontist	(noun) a dentist who specializes in correcting the position of the teeth	61, 111
oust	(verb) to force someone out of a job, position, or competition	35, 60
overt	(adjective) done or shown obviously or publicly; not hidden or secret	38, 85, 123
pachyderm	(noun) a large animal with thick skin (elephant, rhinoceros, or hippopotamus)	26, 136
pack	(verb) to put items into a container; to fill a space; (noun) a group of animals; a number of things grouped together; a backpack	53, 121
pail	(noun) bucket	36
pair	(noun) two things that are intended to be used together; (verb) to make or become one of a pair	9, 40
palate	(noun) the top inside of the mouth; a sense of taste	114
palindrome	(noun) a word or phrase that reads the same backwards as forwards	35, 55
palm	(noun) the part of your hand from your wrist to the fingers; a type of tropical tree with a mass of long pointed leaves at the top	97, 121
panic	(noun) behavior that is sudden, extreme, and results from fear	112
paramedic	(noun) a person who provides emergency medical care	111
paramount	(adjective) more important than anything else	12, 138
passive	(adjective) not involved; not taking part	79
pattern	(noun) repeated arrangement; a design for drawing, sewing, etc.	22
peak	(noun) the top of a mountain; (verb) to reach the highest point	26, 35, 109
pedagogue	(noun) a strict teacher	98
penetrate	(verb) to pass through or into	136
penultimate	(adjective) second from the last	38
peony	(noun) a type of plant with colorful flowers	22
periphery	(noun) the outside edge	84
peril	(noun) danger	112
perilous	(adjective) dangerous	57, 105
perimeter	(noun) the outer edge of an area	95, 136, 138
perish	(verb) to die	17, 91
permanent	(adjective) lasting or intended to last indefinitely; (noun) a hair styling that stays in place	38, 138
permeate	(verb) to spread through something and be present in every part of it	123
permit	(verb) to allow; (noun) an official document that allows you to do something	38, 47
perpetuate	(verb) to cause something to continue	69
perplexed	(adjective) confused, because something is difficult to solve	34, 95
persuade	(verb) to convince people to do or believe something	14, 70
perturbed	(adjective) worried or troubled	82, 134, 136
pester	(verb) to bother someone by asking for something repeatedly	69
petroleum	(noun) an oil obtained from under the ground and made into fuels	91
pharmacist	(noun) someone trained in the preparation of medicines	111
phobia	(noun) an extreme fear or dislike of something	72, 73
phone-	(root) sound; (noun) short form of telephone; (verb) to communicate by telephone	125, 127
photo-	(root) light	125, 127
physician	(noun) a medical doctor	111
piccolo	(noun) a small instrument like a flute, that plays high notes	89

Word	Definition	Seen on Pages
pigment	(noun) a substance that gives something its color	101
pine	(noun) an evergreen coniferous tree; (verb) to miss or long for something	75
pipette	(noun) a thin glass tube used for measuring or moving a small amount of liquid	89
piquant	(adjective) having a sharp, pleasant taste or flvor	114
pique	(verb) to excite or cause interest; (noun) anger or annoyance	91
pirouette	(noun) in ballet, the act of spinning on one foot	9, 105
piscine	(adjective) of, or relating to fish	9
pitch	(verb) to throw something out; to raise a tent and fix it in place; to fall suddenly; (noun) a degree of sound quality; a speech that attempts to persuade someone to buy or do something; the degree of a slope; a sports field	83
placid	(adjective) calm and peaceful	56, 101
plethora	(noun) a large amount of something; excess; abundance	109
pliable	(adjective) easily bent without breaking or cracking; easily influenced or controlled by others	109
pliers	(noun) a small tool used for pulling, holding, or cutting	89
plumber	(noun) someone who supplies, connects, and repairs water pipes and devices	111
pod	(noun) a long seed container that grows on some plants; a group of whales	38, 53
polish	(verb) to shine by rubbing; (noun) a cream that is used to shine something; (adjective) belonging to, or relating to the country of Poland	47
poly-	(root) many	125, 127
pool	(noun) an area of still water; a swimming pool; an amount of money or a number of people or things collected together; a game of billiards (verb) to combine your money with other people for a shared use	53
poise	(noun) behavior or a way of moving that shows calm confidence	105
poplar	(noun) a tall, fast-growing tree of north temperate regions	75
porter	(noun) a person whose job is to carry luggage at railways stations, airports and hotels	111
postpone	(verb) to delay an event or arrange for it to take place at a later time	56
praise	(verb) to express strong admiration for something	12
precipitation	(noun) rain, sleet or snow	9, 56, 96
present	(noun) a gift; this period of time, now; (adjective) in a particular place; (verb) to give, show, provide, or make known; to cause something; to introduce a person	47
priceless	(adjective) treasured, so valuable no price can be assigned	19
prickly	(adjective) having sharp points that stick out; unfriendly and easily annoyed	96
pride	(noun) feelings of your own worth and respect for yourself; a group of lions	53, 121
primary	(adjective) more important than anything else; main; relating to the first part of a child's education; happening first; (noun) an election where political parties decide who will be the candidates in the main election	109, 135
prime	(adjective) most important, or of the best quality; (verb) to prepare someone or something; (noun) the period in your life or your job when you are most active or successful; in math, a whole number greater than 1 whose only factors are 1 and itself	63
principal	(adjective) first in order of importance; (noun) the person in charge at a school; an amount of money that is lent, borrowed, or invested	35, 45, 135
principle	(noun) a moral rule or standard of good behavior; a basic truth that explains how something works	45, 61, 135
priority	(noun) something that is considered more important than other matters	14, 91
prodigy	(noun) a child who shows a great ability at a young age	34
produce	(verb) to create something; to bring something out and show it; to cause a reaction; (noun) food raised through farming (fruits and vegetables)	47

Word	Definition	Seen on Pages
profile	(noun) a side view of a person's face; a description of someone; the amount of public attention someone is receiving; (verb) to write or publish a short description of someone's life	130, 132
progress	(noun) movement to a better position or state, or forward	12, 13, 63
prohibit	(verb) to forbid by law or authority; prevent, not allow	9, 105
prolific	(adjective) producing a great number or amount of something	123
prominent	(adjective) important, famous; sticks out and can be easily seen	134
promote	(verb) to support or actively encourage something; to raise someone to a higher position or grade	84
prompt	(adjective) done quickly; (verb) to cause someone to say or do something	63
proper	(adjective) suitable; correct; according to socially accepted standards	69
protrude	(verb) to stick out	136
prudence	(noun) the quality of having good judgement; cautiousness	98
pseudo	(adjective) not genuine, pretend; (noun) an insincere person	99
pulsate	(verb) to throb, beat or move with a strong, regular rhythm	56, 136
pungent	(adjective) a very strong, sometimes unpleasant smell or taste	56
puny	(adjective) small and weak	32
quay	(noun) a platform extending into the water for loading and unloading ships; dock; pier	9
query	(noun) a question; (verb) to ask questions	87
queue	(noun) a line of people or things waiting for something	97
quiver	(verb) to shake; tremble; (noun) a long, thin container for carrying arrows	53
rabble	(noun) a large, noisy, uncontrolled group of people	87
radiant	(adjective) shining or glowing brightly	30
raise	(verb) to lift up or become higher; to make something bigger or stronger; to take care of children until they have grown; to bring about; (noun) an increase in money earned	9, 41
ramble	(verb) to walk for pleasure; to talk or write in a confused way	101
racquet	(noun) sports equipment used to strike a ball	22
rare	(adjective) not common or frequent; very unusual	82, 133
ravenous	(adjective) extremely hungry	96
ray	(noun) a narrow beam of light, heat, or energy; a slight amount or signal of something good	9, 41
raw	(adjective) uncooked; sore because the skin has been rubbed; cold and wet	67, 121
reach	(verb) to arrive somewhere; to go higher; to stretch out an arm to get or touch something; to communicate with someone, usually by phone	38, 99
real estate	(noun) property in the form of land or buildings	111
rebuke	(verb) to criticize someone strongly; (noun) a reprimand; scolding	56
receptionist	(noun) someone who works in an office, store, etc., helping visitors or giving information	111
rectify	(verb) to correct or make right	69
reel	(noun) a cylinder for winding thread, film, wire, etc. around	43
reform	(verb) to become better, or to make something better; (noun) an improvement	133
refuse	(verb) to not accept, to say no; (noun) unwanted waste; garbage	47
regard	(verb) to consider or have an opinion about something or someone; to look carefully at something or someone	24, 73, 82
regression	(noun) return to a former, less developed state; get worse	12
reign	(verb) to rule a country, or to have power or control; (noun) the period of time when a king or queen rules a country	63
reinforce	(verb) to strengthen or support	13, 91
reliable	(adjective) dependable; can be trusted	69

Word	Definition	Seen on Pages
relinquish	(verb) to give up something; to stop holding or keeping something	135
remnant	(noun) left over piece (usually cloth)	22
remote	(adjective) far away in distance, time, or relation; not close	112
renovate	(verb) to repair and improve something	85
replica	(noun) an exact copy	12
reptile	(noun) cold-blooded animal whose body is covered by scales (snake, crocodile, etc)	26
rescue	(verb) to save someone from a dangerous situation; (noun) the act of being rescued	90
resolve	(verb) to solve a problem; to make a determined decision; (noun) strong determination	55
residence	(noun) the place where someone lives; a home	95
restrict	(verb) to limit someone's actions or movement, or limit the amount or size of something	79, 112
resume	(verb) to start something again after a pause; (noun) a written statement of a person's educational and work experience	25, 47
reveal	(verb) to make known or show something	133, 138
revolt	(verb) to take violent action against authority, to fight or protest; to make someone feel disgusted; (noun) an attempt to overthrow a government by using violence	91
rhododendron	(noun) a flowering shrub	22
rigid	(adjective) not able to be changed or persuaded; stiff or fixed; not able to be bent	38, 72, 121
robust	(adjective) strong and healthy, vigorous; strong and rich in flavor or smell	82, 101
role	(noun) the function or part played by a person in a situation; an actor's part	45
rotten	(adjective) bad; decayed	38, 69
rumor	(noun) a story or report of uncertain or doubtful truth; gossip	75, 112, 113
rupture	(verb) to break or burst suddenly	9
rural	(adjective) of or relating to the country	136
rye	(noun) grain used to feed animals and make bread	45, 60
sabotage	(verb) to intentionally damage or ruin	17
salamander	(noun) a lizard-like amphibian with an elongated body, tail and short limbs	85
saline	(adjective) containing salt; (noun) a mixture of salt and water	63
salvation	(noun) saving someone or something from harm, or from an unpleasant situation	19
sanctuary	(noun) protection or a safe place; part of a church where certain ceremonies take place	95
sanguine	(adjective) positive and hopeful	11
sarcasm	(noun) the use of irony to mock, hurt one's feelings or criticize in a humorous way	91
saunter	(verb) to walk in a slow, relaxed manner	9, 109
scalpel	(noun) small, sharp knife used by a surgeon during an operation	89
scent	(noun) the smell left by a person, animal, perfume, etc.	43, 107
scone	(noun) a small unsweetened or lightly sweetened cake	37
scar	(noun) a mark left on the skin by a cut or burn that has healed; (verb) to leave a scar	99
scope	(noun) the range of matters considered or dealt with; a device for looking at small or far away things; (root) see	125, 127
scorching	(adjective) very hot (weather)	67
scrawny	(adjective) thin and bony	102
scruffy	(adjective) untidy, dirty	77
searing	(adjective) very hot (weather); very powerful, extreme (pain)	67
secure	(adjective) free from risk; confident; fixed, locked into a position; (verb) to obtain; to fasten; to make safe	83
sedentary	(adjective) involving little movement or physical activity	123
seize	(verb) to take possession of something; to take by force	87
seldom	(adverb) almost never; rarely	60
serenade	(verb) to play music or sing for someone, especially romantically	72, 73

Word	Definition	Seen on Pages
series	(noun) a number of similar or related things; a set of books or TV programs	22
settle	(verb) to reach an agreement; to pay a debt	38, 134, 139
sever	(verb) to separate or break something, especially by cutting	63
severe	(adjective) causing great pain, difficulty, or damage; not kind or sympathetic; harsh	55, 60
shabby	(adjective) looking old and in bad condition because of wear	77, 107
sham	(noun) someone or something that is fake with intent to deceive; (adjective) not real	61, 84
shawl	(noun) a large scarf used to cover the head and shoulders; cloak	22
shelter	(noun) a place that provides protection; (verb) to protect yourself or someone else, against a person, bad weather, danger, etc.	83, 85
shin pad	(noun) hard plastic worn inside a sock to protect the lower leg (hockey, football, etc)	22
shoot	(verb) to fire a gun or weapon; (in sports) to throw, kick or hit a ball toward a goal; to film or photograph something; (noun) the first part of a plant to appear above the ground	45
shortage	(noun) situation where not enough of something can be obtained; scarcity	105
shrewd	(adjective) showing good judgement; clever	138
shroud	(noun) cover; a cloth in which a person is wrapped for burial; (verb) to cover	14, 91
shun	(verb) to avoid or refuse to accept someone or something	77
signify	(verb) to mean something; to make known	105
similar	(adjective) looking alike or being almost the same	70
sizzling	(adverb) very hot	67
sketch	(noun) a quick drawing; a short description that does not give many details; a short, humorous performance (TV, radio, etc); (verb) to quickly make a simple drawing	77, 107
slab	(noun) a thick, flat, usually square or rectangular piece of a solid substance	36
slander	(noun) the act of making false statements about a person to damage their reputation	133
slate	(noun) a dark gray rock; the people who are trying to be elected; (verb) to schedule or expect to happen	53
sleek	(adjective) smooth and glossy; having an elegant, streamlined shape or design	102
sleet	(noun) wet, partly melted falling snow	9, 96
slumber	(verb) to sleep	133
snob	(noun) a person with an exaggerated respect for high social position or wealth	34
snooty	(adjective) self-important; seeming to think one is better than everyone else	34
soaked	(adjective) extremely wet	70
solemn	(adjective) serious and without any humor	109
solid	(adjective) firm, not liquid; dense; strong; certain; (noun) food that is not liquid; a shape with 3 dimensions; (adverb) full	83
sombrero	(noun) a wide-brimmed hat, especially worn in Mexico and the southwestern US	26
soprano	(noun) a woman's or young boy's singing voice in the highest range	89
sound	(noun) something you can hear; a noise; a passage connecting two seas; (verb) to make a noise; to seem; (adjective) in good condition; solid; good	9, 38, 61, 83, 121, 127
spectrum	(noun) a band of colors as seen in a rainbow; a continuous range or sequence	9, 91
sphere	(noun) a solid shape like a round ball; a subject or area of knowledge; (root) ball	87, 125, 127
spoil	(verb) to destroy or damage; food going bad; to treat someone very or too well	38, 98
spread	(verb) to open out something so as to extend its surface area, width, or length; extend over a large area; (noun) the process of spreading out; the extent of area covered by something	99, 123
spry	(adjective) active and able to move quickly	60
spruce	(noun) an evergreen tree with thin, pointed leaves; (verb) to make something tidy	75
spur	(verb) to encourage an activity; to cause something to develop faster	35

Word	Definition	Seen on Pages
squabble	(noun) a disagreement, often about an unimportant matter; (verb) to argue over something not important	69
squander	(verb) to waste money, or use something in a foolish way	79
squeal	(verb) to make a long, very high sound or cry	69
squeamish	(adjective) easily upset by things one finds unpleasant	69
stagehand	(noun) someone who moves the scenery and props during a play	8
stallion	(noun) an adult male horse	26
steadfast	(adjective) staying the same for a long time; not changing or losing purpose	61
stenographer	(noun) a person who does shorthand in an office or records speech using a special machine in a court	111
stethoscope	(noun) a medical device that allows a doctor to listen to your heart	89
stimulating	(adjective) causing interest or enthusiasm	95
strategy	(noun) a plan of action designed to achieve a goal	13, 91
stretch	(verb) to make longer or wider without tearing or breaking; to extend part of one's body to the fullest length; (noun) the act of stretching one's body; a continuous area or expanse of land or water	99
strife	(noun) bitter disagreement, conflict, dispute	9, 91
stringent	(adjective) extremely limiting or difficult; severe	123
strut	(verb) to walk proudly or arrogantly, trying to look important; (noun) a support for a structure such as an aircraft wing, roof, or bridge	38, 55
sturdy	(adjective) strongly built	14
sub-	(noun) a replacement; a ship (submarine); a sandwich; (root) under	125, 127
subject	(noun) topic; an area of knowledge studied in a course; the thing being considered; a person who lives in or who has the right to live in a particular country; (verb) to defeat people or a country and then control them	121, 132
subsequent	(adjective) happening after something else; following	77
substitute	(verb) to use one thing instead of another; to replace; (noun) a replacement	135
subtly	(adverb) in a way that is small and difficult to notice or describe	130, 132
sufficient	(adjective) having enough; adequate	105
sultry	(adjective) very hot and humid	67
summit	(noun) the highest point of something, like a mountain; an important meeting	12, 60
surplus	(noun) an amount that is more than needed	12, 91
suspicion	(noun) a feeling that something is likely or true; the belief that someone is guilty of something; lack of belief in someone or something; doubt	133
swarm	(noun) a large group of insects, or any large, busy group; (verb) to move in a large group	9, 53
sweeping	(adjective) having great effect or range	83
sweltering	(adjective) extremely hot	67
swift	(adjective) moving at great speed; fast; (noun) a small type of bird	57
swindle	(verb) to steal; (noun) a fraudulent scheme or action	14
swollen	(adjective) larger than usual	81
symbol	(noun) a sign, shape, or object used to represent something else	38, 45
syn-	(root) same	125, 127
syringe	(noun) a tube for collecting blood or injecting other liquids, usually with a needle	89
tablet	(noun) a pill; a piece of stone used for writing (in ancient times); a drawing pad; a small flat computer that uses a touch screen or pen to operate	56
taboo	(noun) something that is avoided or forbidden for religious or social reasons	91
tactful	(adjective) showing skill in dealing with others; considerate, thoughtful	9

Word	Definition	Seen on Pages
tailgate	(verb) to drive too closely behind another vehicle; to have an informal party with food served from the back of a car	8
tailor	(noun) someone whose job is to make, repair, and adjust clothes; (verb) to adjust something to suit a particular need or situation	99, 111
talon	(noun) a claw belonging to a bird of prey	72, 73
tambourine	(noun) an instrument resembling a shallow drum with metal discs in slots around the edge, played by being shaken or hit with the hand	26
tame	(adjective) not wild or fierce; (verb) to make a wild animal tame; to control something	35
tang	(noun) a sharp, distinctive taste	114
tardy	(adjective) late in arriving or happening	69
tarmac	(noun) material used to surface roads and other outdoor areas; the areas of an airport where aircraft take off, land and park	60
tart	(adjective) tasting sour; (noun) a small pastry with a usually sweet filling	37
teak	(noun) a large tropical tree; the wood of a teak tree	85
teal	(noun) a small wild duck; a dark greenish-blue color	26, 36
tear	(noun) a drop of water from the eyes when crying; (verb) to pull apart	47, 121
temperate	(adjective) not extreme; within a middle range	67
template	(noun) a pattern used to make copies of a shape or help cut materials accurately; something that is used as a pattern for producing other similar things	56
temporary	(adjective) not lasting; not permanent	80, 138
tender	(adjective) gentle, caring, or sympathetic; painful or sore; easily cut or chewed; (verb) to offer something, usually in writing; (noun) a formal offer, usually to buy something	38
tense	(adjective) anxious, unable to relax; tight and stiff	38
tension	(noun) the state of being stretched tight; mental and emotional strain	70, 134
tentative	(adjective) not certain or confident	38, 56
tepee	(noun) a cone-shaped tent	55, 85
tepid	(adjective) not very warm; not very strong; not enthusiastic	60, 67
textile	(noun) a cloth made by hand or machine	11, 22
theater	(noun) a place where people can watch a performance, a movie, or another activity	56
thimble	(noun) a small metal cap to protect the finger while sewing	22
thrifty	(adjective) being very careful with money, avoiding waste	38
thwart	(verb) to keep something from happening	12, 91
tidy	(adjective) everything in order, neat; (of amounts of money) large	12, 132
timpani	(noun) large metal drums with round bottoms played in an orchestra	89
toil	(noun) hard and tiring work; (verb) to work hard	60
tolerate	(verb) to allow the existence of something; endure; permit	13, 109
tonic	(noun) a liquid medicine intended to make you feel better	60
torrential	(adjective) used to refer to very heavy rain	133
torment	(noun) great mental or physical suffering; (verb) to cause someone to suffer or worry	60, 79
torso	(noun) the main part of the body between the waist and neck	55
trampoline	(noun) gym equipment that you jump up and down on	22
trance	(noun) a half-conscious state, where one is not in control of themselves	95
tranquil	(adjective) peaceful; calm	9, 14
tranquility	(noun) state of being calm and peaceful	69
transcribe	(verb) to make a complete written record of spoken or written words	111
translator	(noun) person who changes one language into another	32
transparent	(adjective) something that can be seen through; obvious; open and honest	130, 132, 136

Word	Definition	Seen on Pages
triangle	(noun) a flat shape with three straight sides; a triangular-shaped musical instrument that is played by striking it with a metal bar	89
trio	(noun) a group of three people or things	9
trivial	(adjective) of little importance	14, 107
tropical	(adjective) of or characteristic of the tropics; extremely hot	67, 97
trout	(noun) a type of fresh water fish	22
trove	(noun) a collection of valuable things	35, 95
turbulent	(adjective) moving very strongly and suddenly; full of confusion; lacking order	100, 138
turncoat	(noun) a traitor; one who deserts a cause for the other side	8
turnkey	(adjective) service that is ready for immediate use	8
tutor	(noun) a private teacher; (verb) to teach a student privately	123
umpire	(noun) in some sports, a person who makes sure that the rules are followed; a referee	55
unanimous	(adjective) in complete agreement or showing complete agreement; supported by all	56
unearth	(verb) to discover; find something in the ground by digging	95
unforeseen	(adjective) not expected or predicted	135
uni-	(root) one	125, 127
unpalatable	(adjective) unpleasant to taste or eat; difficult to accept	72, 73
unravel	(verb) to separate cloth into threads; to solve a crime or explain a mystery; to destroy a process or achievement	109
unruly	(adjective) difficult to control or manage	109
upholstery	(noun) padding for furniture, such as armchairs and sofas	11
urge	(verb) to encourage someone strongly to do something; (noun) a strong desire	35
urn	(noun) a large container, round on one stem; vase	55
vague	(adjective) unclear, not clearly stated or defined	24, 70, 84
vain	(adjective) having a high opinion of one's own appearance or abilities	34
valiant	(adjective) showing courage or determination	32
vanish	(verb) to disappear suddenly	131, 132
vast	(adjective) extremely large; enormous	61
ventilator	(noun) a device that allows fresh air to come into a closed space; a machine that helps people breathe by allowing air to flow in and out of their lungs	89
vertebrate	(noun) an animal that has a spine or backbone	55
vertical	(adjective) standing or pointing straight up or at a 90 degree angle	70, 98
vex	(verb) to annoy or to cause someone to feel angry	107
vibration	(noun) the action of shaking or quivering	114
vice	(noun) a tool with two parts that tightens to hold objects in order to work on them; immoral behavior; (prefix) used as part of a title usually designating as second in charge	89
vicious	(adjective) deliberately cruel or violent	34
vie	(verb) to compete with other people to achieve or win something	38
vigilance	(noun) the state of keeping careful watch out for danger	98
villain	(noun) a bad person; a criminal; an evil or cruel character in a story	56
violin	(noun) a wooden musical instrument played by moving a bow across the strings	89
volatile	(adjective) likely to change suddenly, and become violent or angry	104
voluntary	(adjective) without being forced or paid to do it	91
waive	(verb) to give up a right to something; forfeit	45
walnut	(noun) the large wrinkled edible seed of the walnut tree; a tall tree which produces walnuts, with compound leaves and valuable ornamental timber	75

Word	Definition	Seen on Pages
warp	(verb) to bend or twist a material so it is no longer straight; (noun) a twist or distortion in the shape of something	82
wave	(verb) to greet, moving your hand; to move something from side to side (like a flag); (noun) a raised movement of water on the surface; a sudden increase in an activity	45
whetted	(past tense of whet) sharpened	96
wholesome	(adjective) good for you; healthy	79
willow	(noun) a tree or shrub of temperate climates which typically has narrow leaves, and grows near water	75
wind	(noun) movement of air; (verb) to twist something around something; to follow a route that bends or curves repeatedly	53, 100, 116, 131
witness	(verb) to see an event; (noun) someone who has seen something, usually a crime	114
wound	(noun) a hurt or injury; (verb) to hurt or injure someone; (past tense - wind)	47
wrap	(verb) to cover or surround something; (noun) material that is used to cover or protect something; a piece of clothing worn on the shoulders	83
wry	(adjective) showing that you find a bad situation funny	45
x-ray	(noun) a type of radiation that can go through many solid substances, allowing hidden objects such as bones in the body to be photographed	89
yew	(noun) a coniferous tree which has red berrylike fruits, and most parts of which are highly poisonous.	75
yoke	(noun) a wooden bar fastened over the necks of two animals and connected to a vehicle or load that they are pulling	45
yolk	(noun) the yellow part of an egg	45, 55
zenith	(noun) point at which something is the most powerful or successful; pinnacle	19

ANSWER KEY

Missing Link, page 8
1) boy 2) house 3) room 4) line 5) mail 6) fore 7) water 8) tower 9) case 10) skin 11) dress 12) hand 13) gate 14) down 15) coat 16) chair 17) fish 18) key 19) fly 20) guard, 21) bill 22) ball

Analogies, page 9
1) sound 2) flotilla 3) feline 4) fourteen 5) rush 6) rays 7) prohibit 8) leisurely 9) break 10) clear 11) light 12) narrow 13) dance 14) blue 15) millennium 16) hive 17) harp 18) snow 19) communication 20) duo

You're Breaking Up, pages 10-11
Answers: CACOPHONY, UPHOLSTERY, CATALOG, INNOCULATE, BAROMETER, EXTINCT, TEXTILES, COPYRIGHT, BOUYANT, MENTALLY, SANGUINE

Fake News, pages 12-13
1) original, deceitful 2) endangered, anxious 3) loyalty 4) paramount 5) tidy, overjoyed 6) thwarted, summit 7) progress 8) surplus 9) praised 10) dusk 11) expansion 12) decade 13) lofty 14) tolerate 15) formidable 16) reinforced 17) strategy 18) encouraged 19) realistic 20) exaggerate

Word Search I – Synonyms, pages 14-15

CHEAT – SWINDLE
PERSUADE – COAX
NEXT TO – ADJACENT
GAIN – BENEFIT
A PRICE ESTIMATE
UNIMPORTANT – TRIVIAL
EXAMINE IN DETAIL – ANALYZE
UGLY – GROTESQUE
COVER – SHROUD
MORE IMPORTANT – PRIORITY
MAYHEM – CHAOS
WELL BUILT – STURDY
MODEST – HUMBLE
TO SUPPLY WATER TO – IRRIGATE
JOKER – JESTER
BLACK – EBONY
PEACEFUL – TRANQUIL
LUXURIOUS – LAVISH
STARTING POINT – ORIGIN
FIERCE – FEROCIOUS

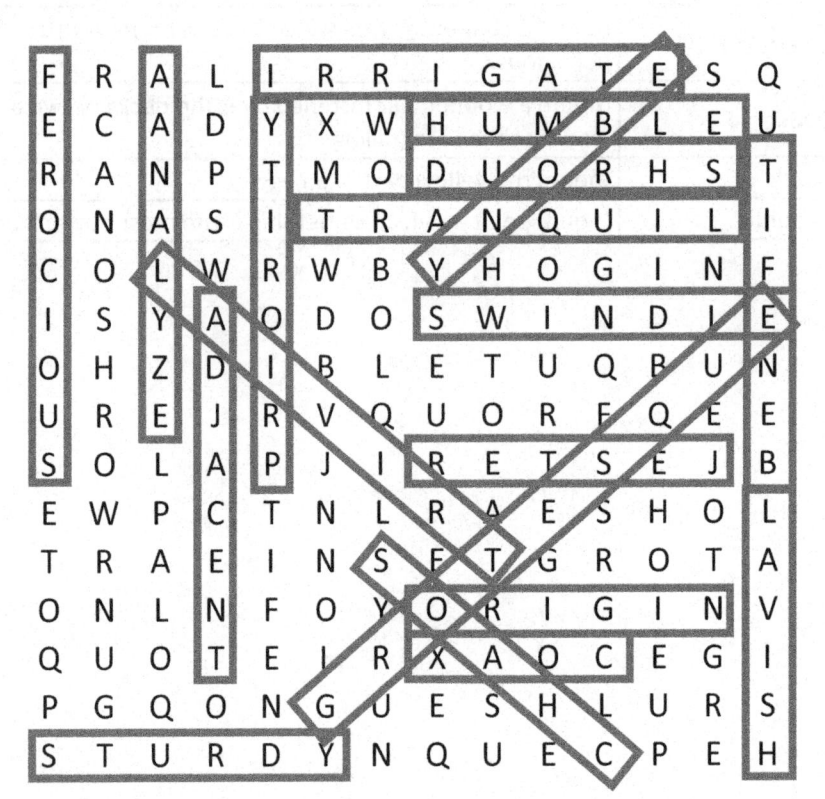

Shop 'Til You Drop!, pages 22-23
<u>Jazz's Jewellery</u>: BROOCH, LOCKET, CUFFLINKS; <u>Fiona's Fashions</u>: SHAWL, GOWN, CRAVAT, BERET; <u>Fantastic Fish Market</u>: HADDOCK, TROUT, BASS, COD; <u>Fabulous Furniture</u>: FUTON, BUREAU, ARMOIRE, HUTCH; <u>Flo's Flowers</u>: BEGONIA, PEONY, DAISY, RHODODDENDRON; <u>Bountiful Books</u>: ANTHOLOGY, AUTOBIOGRAPHY, SERIES, ENCYCLOPEDIA; <u>Sewing Shop</u>: THIMBLE, TEXTILES, REMNANTS, PATTERNS; <u>Sporting Goods</u>: TRAMPOLINE, RACQUET, GOGGLES, SHIN PADS

Synonyms In The Wild, page 24-25
1) DUBIOUSLY, 2) VAGUE, 3) INGRATIATING, 4) CORRESPONDING, 5) AUSPICIOUSLY,
6) FACETIOUS, 7) AWKWARD, 8) MENACING, 9) FOREBODINGS, 10) DISSIPATED 11) COY

Where Am I?, pages 26-29
HELIX – C8, FLOTILLA – C4, FOLIAGE – A5, HYDRANT – A8, FELINE – A2, PEAK – B5, PACHYDERM – C3, FOUNDRY – A6, REPTILE – C7, BANNER – C9, AMPHIBIAN – C2, CREEK – A1, TAMBOURINE – B8, HADDOCK – A3, MANOR – B2, IMP – C6, DINGHY – C1, TEAL – B9, MACE – B6, SOMBRERO – C5, BOVINE – B1, CANINE – A4, STALLION – A7, FORTRESS – B7

BONUS: The Dromedary is in B4. The two-humped camel in B3 is called a Bactrian Camel.

Fill In The Blanks, page 35
1) stop / open 2) cape / peak 3) flex / exit 4) east / still 5) sofa / fact 6) tame / mend 7) trove / oven 8) launch / chide 9) spur / urge 10) gauntlet / letter 11) civil / illegal 12) balmy / myriad 13) affluent / entrance 14) constant / antagonize 15) nimble / blender 16) principal / palindrome 17) auspicious / ousted 18) disobey / beyond 19) chaperone / onerous 20) economical / callous   21) camouflage / agenda

Word Ladders, pages 36-37
1) FOX – FOG – FIG – DIG
2) CATS – CARS – CARP – HARP
3) BALL – FALL – FAIL – PAIL
4) TEAM – TEAL – TELL – SELL
5) CRAM – CLAM – SLAM – SLAB
6) WELD – HELD – HERD – HERO
7) WORM – FORM – FARM – HARM – HART – CART – TART
8) CLAP – CLIP – SLIP – SLIT – SLOT – SHOT – SHOP
9) SCORE – SCONE – STONE – STORE – STARE – START – SMART
10) CRANE – CRAVE – GRAVE – GLADE – BLADE – BLAME – FLAME – FLAKE

Crossword, pages 38-39

	P	E	N	U	L	T	I	M	A	T	E		E	C	H	O
E		O		E		G		S						A	
R	O	T	T	E	N		G	E	N	T	L	E		B	
M		E		T		N		E		L	A		I	
I	C	O	N		A	D	V	E	R	S	I	T	Y
T		D	A	T	E		A	I	M		Y		A	
	V		E		I			E		N		A	T	E
D	E	P	R	I	V	E	S			O				M
	R				E	X	I	T		N				I
T		L	O	B		C		R	E	A	C	H		G
H	O	A	X			A		U			H		M	A	R
R		M		O		V	O	T	E		A		E		A
I	R	E		P	E	A			G	A	L	L	A	N	T
F		N		E	A	T	I	N	G		A		G		E
T		T	E	N	S	E		O		N	E	E	D	
Y	E	S		T		A	D	O	P	T		R	

171

Same But Different, page 47
1) content 2) tear 3) refuse 4) close 5) invalid 6) object 7) permit 8) wound 9) resume 10) console 11) polish 12) present 13) excuse 14) contest 15) produce

Collective Clues, page 53
army of ants; **pack** of wolves; **pride** of lions; **pod** of whales; **litter** of puppies; **murder** of crows, **nest** of vipers, **host** of angels, **slate** of candidates, **orchestra** of crickets, **arsenal** of guns, **barrel** of laughs, **quiver** of arrows, **bed** of oysters, **pool** of typists, **swarm** of mosquitoes, **index** of names, **clutch** of eggs

Spreading The Word, pages 60-61
1) spry 2) lodge 3) oust 4) toil 5) seldom 6) expand 7) martyr 8) summit 9) wit 10) omit 11) tepid 12) import 13) oath 14) limb 15) kindle 16) sham 17) vast 18) immerse 19) din 20) malady 21) astute 22) grimace 23) heir 24) donation 25) chord 26) neon 27) idle 28) moral 29) anchor 30) debrief 31) steadfast 32) coy

The Heat is On, pages 66-68
Multiple answers, one suggested order : (Hottest to Coldest): scorching, searing, sizzling, sweltering, tropical, sultry, baking, humid, balmy, temperate, mild, tepid, lukewarm, inclement, nippy, chilly, freezing, icy, bitter, frigid, raw, biting

Word Search II Antonyms, pages 70-71

HISTORIC - OBSCURE
VERTICAL - HORIZONTAL
UNMANAGEABLE - OBEDIENT
BOLSTER - EXHAUST
MILD - DRASTIC
DIFFERENT - SIMILAR
LOSE - ACQUIRE
TINY - MASSIVE
PEACEFUL - BELLIGERENT
SOAKED - ARID
CONFRONT = **AVOID**
ESTABLISH - ABOLISH
VAGUE - ACCURATE
ALERT - DROWSY
COWARDLY - HEROIC
HARMONY - TENSION
UNKNOWN - FAMILIAR
DISCOURAGE - PERSUADE
FAKE - GENUINE
INCLUDE – OMIT

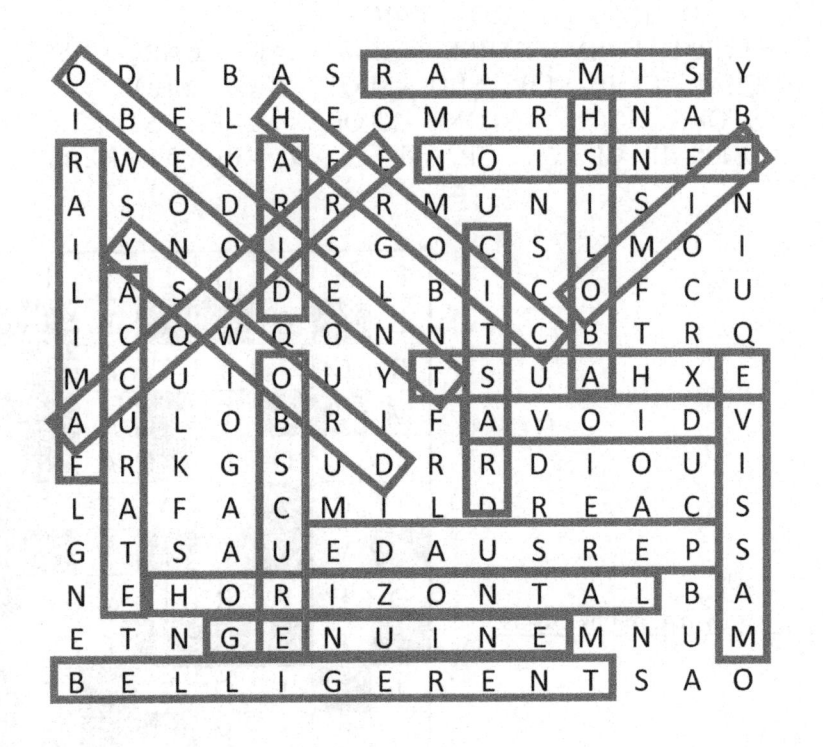

Hidden Among the Trees, page 75
The trees are: APPLE, ASH, ASPEN, BEECH, BIRCH, CHERRY, DOGWOOD, ELM, FIR, HICKORY, JUNIPER, MAGNOLIA, MAPLE, OAK, PINE, POPLAR, SPRUCE, WALNUT, WILLOW, YEW

Dial A Clue, pages 76-77

donate = **GIVE**, debate = **TALK**, interval = **BREAK**, ajar = **OPEN**,
scruffy = **SHABBY**, contemporary = **MODERN**, delayed = **LATE**, sketch = **DRAW**,
fret = **WORRY**, labyrinth = **MAZE**, agile = **NIMBLE**, avoid = **SHUN**,
foundation = **BASE**, subsequent = **NEXT**, cruel = **UNKIND**, combine = **BLEND**,
dozen = **TWELVE**

Synonym Maze, page 83

COMMENCE
LAUNCH
PITCH
SOUND
SOLID
SECURE
SHELTER
COVER
CONCEAL
CAMOUFLAGE
MASK
CLOAK
WRAP
BLANKET
SWEEPING
ENTIRE
EXHAUSTIVE
TOTAL
COMPREHENSIVE
COMPLETE
END

Odd One Out, pages 84-85

1) clarify 2) beret 3) capable 4) nylon 5) erratic 6) idle 7) originate 8) ominous 9) periphery
10) discourage 11) elderly 12) nail 13) limb 14) incision 15) salamander 16) renovate
17) television 18) discuss 19) cravat 20) teak 21) baguette 22) chief 23) obscure 24) contract

Being Instrumental, page 89

<u>HOSPITAL</u>: STETHOSCOPE, SCALPEL, FORCEPS, SYRINGE, PIPETTE, X-RAY, VENTILATOR
<u>CONCERT HALL</u>: SOPRANO, BASSOON, CYMBALS, PICCOLO, TRIANGLE, CASTANETS, VIOLIN, TIMPANI <u>FACTORY</u>: VICE, JIGSAW, CHISEL, ANVIL, PLIERS

Nonsense Poetry, page 97

This section uses homophones and alternate meanings for a bit of humor: dual (duel); desert (dessert); cops (copse); flea (flee); bald (bawled); cue (queue); bow (bough), colonel (kernel); feet (feat); palm (tropical tree); friendly drink (cordial); harp (musical instrument & to dwell on tiresomely); die (singular of dice)

Hidden Link, pages 98-99
1) Lecturer (UNIVERSITY) 2) Caution (CONSIDERATION) 3) Spoil (SCAR)
4) Adapt (MORPH) 5) Reach (DISTANCE) 6) Anonymous (INTRIGUE)

Missing Word Sentences, page 102-103
1) embezzled 2) economize 3) guarantee 4) sleek 5) ceased 6) obvious
7) chaotic 8) abandon 9) gullible 10) decay 11) adversity 12) ebb
13) exterior 14) frequent 15) caricatures 16) scrawny 17) fortunate 18) assembled
19) immense 20) casual

Professionally Speaking, page 111
Makes maps – CARTOGRAPHER

Studies the economy – ECONOMIST

Makes arrangements at a funeral – MORTICIAN

Sells houses and property – REAL ESTATE AGENT

Handles and carries luggage – PORTER

Doctor – PHYSICIAN

Greets clients at an office – RECEPTIONIST

Digs up and studies artifacts – ARCHAEOLOGIST

Fixes leaks – PLUMBER

Designs machines or structures – ENGINEER

Designs buildings – ARCHITECT

Helps to straighten teeth – ORTHODONTIST

Provides emergency medical care – PARAMEDIC

Practices law in a court – ATTORNEY

Makes and repairs clothing – TAILOR

Dispenses medicine – PHARMACIST

Fits glass into windows and doors – GLAZIER

Makes and repairs things in iron – BLACKSMITH

A person who gives beauty treatments – COSMETOLOGIST

Makes and repairs wooden objects – CARPENTER

Expert on diet and nutrition – DIETICIAN

A person who transcribes speech in shorthand – STENOGRAPHER

Makes shoes for horses – FARRIER

Whale of a Tale, pages 112-113
1) calamities 2) fortitude 3) exaggerate 4) rumors
5) adequate 6) circulate 7) hereditary 8) remotest
9) latitudes 10) morbid 11) panic 12) perils

Word Search III Senses, pages 114-115

	SMELL	HEAR	TASTE	FEEL	SEE
1. AROMA	X				
2. CONTACT				X	
3. PIQUANT			X		
4. CACOPHONY		X			
5. GRAZE				X	
6. WITNESS					X
7. FRAGRANT	X				
8. EAVESDROP		X			
9. CARESS				X	
10. STENCH	X				
11. PALATE			X		
12. VIBRATION		X		X	X
13. DETECT	X	X	X	X	X
14. BOUQUET	X				
15. HARK		X			
16. TANG			X		

Anagrams, page 123

1) ANECDOTE   2) AVARICE   3) OVERT   4) LENIENT   5) APATHY   6) TUTOR
7) STRINGENT   8) SEDENTARY   9) IMPECCABLE   10) INCITE   11) CALLOUS
12) PERMEATE   13) CANDOR   14) PROLIFIC   15) GREGARIOUS

Out of Time, pages 130-132

1) mechanism   2) profile   3) adroitly   4) apparatus   5) interminable   6) subtly   7) framework
8) indistinct   9) mantel   10) transparent   11) explicit   12) illuminated   13) askew   14) vanish

Idioms, page 133

Once in a blue moon - Something that occurs very rarely; Let the cat out of the bag - Reveal a secret; Hold your tongue - Remain silent; Go cold turkey - Stop or quit a habit suddenly; Smell a rat - Have a suspicion something is wrong; Mind your Ps & Qs - Be on your best behavior; Sling mud - To slander or insult someone; A feather in your cap - An achievement; Have your heart in your mouth - To be worried or frightened; Catch 40 winks – Slumber; Take the bull by the horns - To directly confront a difficult situation; Pull the wool over someone's eyes - To deceive someone; Turn over a new leaf - Reform; Sit on the fence - Delay making a decision; Pull someone's leg - To deceive playfully, tease; Break a leg - (wishing you) Good Luck; Blow your own horn - Be boastful;

Raining cats and dogs – Torrential; Face the music - Face the consequences; Throw in the towel - To concede, give up; Draw the line - To set boundaries; A piece of cake - Something very easy; Be under the weather - To not feel well

Best Fit, pages 134-135

1)b. mystify   2)c. variety   3)b. exhibition   4)d. adjoining   5)c. complex   6)b. gather   7)a. gallant
8)c. gain   9)d. strain   10)a. conspicuous   11)c. replacement   12)b. predict   13)d. abdicate
14)c. easy   15)b. contradict   16)d. principal   17)c. estimated   18)b. unforeseen   19)a. equal
20)d. suddenly

Dot to Dot, pages 136-137
not transparent = opaque
desire = craving
neutral = indifferent
complain = gripe
worried = perturbed
exaggerate = embellish
careful with money = economical
outside edge = perimeter
untidy = disheveled
magical = enchanting,
throb or move rhythmically = pulsate
to go into = penetrate
difficult to carry = bulky
changeable personality = fickle
stick out = protrude
rude = impertinent
beginner = novice
not urban = rural
go faster = accelerate

Bonus Question: PACHYDERM

Missing Letter Antonyms, page 138
1) drastic - calm   2) assistance - hindrance   3) turbulent - gentle   4) obedient - insolent   5) shrewd - foolish   6) oppress - assist   7) origin - conclusion   8) realistic – impractical   9) inferior – paramount   10) eradicate - construct   11) miniscule - gigantic   12) expansion - contraction   13) temporary – permanent   14) fortify - weaken   15) perimeter - center   16) conceal - reveal   17) hapless - fortunate   18) fantasy - reality

Antonym Maze, page 139
START > FINISH
FINISH > BIRTH
BIRTH > DEATH
DEATH > LIFE
LIFE > LETHARY
LETHARGY > ACTIVE
ACTIVE > IDLE
IDLE > MOBILE
MOBILE > SETTLED
SETTLED > OPEN
OPEN > COMPLETE
COMPLETE > BEGIN
BEGIN > END

Also available from Liz Judge

The Big Logic Puzzle Extravaganza for Gifted & Talented Children

A compilation of logic puzzles to challenge and improve children's problem solving abilities. Particularly useful for gifted and talented children starting from age 9, although all age groups up to adult can enjoy.

Includes: Verbal reasoning, non-verbal reasoning, brain teasers, riddles, worded problems, spatial reasoning questions, mazes, and much more.

Made in the USA
Coppell, TX
23 May 2022